# REFLECTIONS
## DURING A PANDEMIC

*Thoughts While Sheltering in Place*

**Numbered Edition: Copy** 53 **of 200**

Dear Mordechai
Best wishes to you now
And always
Eugene Michael Giudice

## EUGENE MICHAEL GIUDICE

Eugene Michael Giudice

Printed in the United States of America
First Printing 2021
First Edition 2021

ISBN: 978-0-578-78400-7
Library of Congress Control Number: 2020920684

10 9 8 7 6 5 4 3 2 1

Front and back cover art by https://www.fiverr.com/slonelynn

# TABLE OF CONTENTS

# ACKNOWLEDGEMENTS

I have many people to acknowledge and thank for their support in creating the content for this book. As I look back over the past year, it is very apparent that without many people's aid, the content that makes up this book would have never seen the light of day.

None of this would be possible without the love and care shown to me by my parents Rosa and Ennio Giudice. It is through their sweat and tears and risks that they took in leaving a war-ravaged Europe to build a new life in the United States that I have been able to achieve anything, both personally and professionally.

The first person to be thanked is my wife Colleen, whose presence during these past months has been a steadying influence on me and a source of great inspiration and joy. I have always said that my marriage to her was the making of me, and that is so true in the manifestation of this book

Finally, I must acknowledge the support of many friends, both inside and outside the librarian profession, who have called or emailed messages of support and encouragement during the past year. It is their words, their presence, that has permitted me to go on with this effort. I want to mention in particular the people who regularly joined the Tuesday, Wednesday, Thursday or Friday Zoom coffee breaks. These people provided me with unstinting support and encouragement, and through their presence, we, together, built an authentic community.

# PREFACE

These past fourteen months have been significant for many reasons. Not only are we experiencing the continued COVD-19 pandemic, but we have seen tectonic shifts in our political, social, and cultural lives. These events have brought out the best and the worst in many. Patterns of life, business, and education have been disrupted, and this disruption has caused many to lose hope, turn inward and become cynical.

When it became apparent that I, and many others, would be working from home for an extended period, I took it upon myself to send out a periodic email message to friends and colleagues. I started these email messages simply as a means to help give people hope; to let them recapture some of their basic humanity and dignity and maybe, in the process, come to appreciate the humanity and dignity of others.

These messages span a year of sheltering in place. They are by no means a cure for all the ills of society. They are meant to act as a prism through which thoughts and feelings may pass through and emerge as something more vibrant, more meaningful, on which to build a future.

They are humbly offered for your consideration.

**Eugene Michael Giudice**

**June 2021**

# MARCH 2020

Good Morning

Please don't take offense, but I have given myself the task of coming up with a quote and other things that might be worth a minute's thinking about during this extended crisis.

As many of us might find ourselves working alone at home, our sense of isolation may increase. In that spirit, I thought this quote from Golda Meir may be useful to encourage each of us to trust ourselves and use this time to help foster a better sense of who we are and who we want to be.

- **"Trust yourself. Create the kind of self that you will be happy to live with all your life. Make the most of yourself by fanning the tiny, inner sparks of possibility into flames of achievement."**

Eugene

Good Morning Everyone

I've had to do some shopping at Target and Costco recently, and I saw something interesting. I had expected to see hordes of people grabbing everything off the shelves. To be fair, there were items in short supply, but people were not maniacs about it.

It gave me pause to think about my fears and concerns during this time of great uncertainty, so I thought it might help find something from two people who are about as opposite as can be.

The first is from Nelson Mandela. He said the following: **"I learned that courage was not the absence of fear, but the triumph over it. The brave man is not he who does not feel afraid, but he who conquers that fear."** The second is from Pope John XXIII in his address at the opening of the Second Vatican Council. He said this to the council fathers: **"We feel that We must disagree with these prophets of doom, who are always forecasting worse disasters, as though the end of the world were at hand."**

As we all, as a community, move forward, let us not take counsel of our fears. Let us continue to support each other. There are times when each of us will need a little propping up.

Let's be there for each other.

Good Morning Everyone

I came across a note from Edmund Hillary. Here is what he said about having a sense of humor:

**"Good planning is important. I've also regarded a sense of humor as one of the most important things on a big expedition. When you're in a difficult or dangerous situation, or when you're depressed about the chances of success, someone who can make you laugh eases the tension."**

During this time, we (me especially) cannot take ourselves too seriously. We need to find something to chuckle at. Sometimes, we are our own best material in that regard. Who knows, before this crisis ends, I may end up reading the comics on a livestream like New York City Mayor Fiorello LaGuardia.

I had the opportunity to listen via webcam to a sermon given by a priest and friend of mine. His name is Aidan O'Boyle, and he is pastor of St. Muredach's Cathedral in Ballina, County Mayo. He said that the only thing more contagious than a virus is hope, and maybe a close second would be humor.

Good Morning

Have you ever thought that life is like an orange?

First, you have to peel away a lot of stuff to get to the sweetness within, just like life is sometimes. Each orange segment is different, but it makes up one whole orange, just like humanity. You can share the orange segments with others or enjoy them by yourself, just like life.

During this time of working from home and disrupted social and professional networks, please take time to think about finding "your orange" for today … just today and be sure to enjoy it.

That being said, a little more citrus fruit in our lives won't be such a bad thing.

Stay well, stay safe and enjoy the orange you find today.

Eugene

Good Morning

Stephen Covey, the author of *The Seven Habits of Highly Successful People*, said this about trust:

**Trust is the glue of life. It's the most essential ingredient in effective communication. It is the fundamental principle that holds all relationships.**

At this time, we are more dependent on mediated communications (email, phone, online chat). We must rely on others' good faith to help us deliver value. I would submit to you that this trust also needs to extend to trusting our instincts.

I am convinced that by relying on others' good intentions and trusting our wisdom, we will be able to deliver value in the short term, and in the long term, we will be better members of society.

Regards,

Eugene

Good Morning

I'm feeling a little defiant today.

This put me in mind of Anthony McAuliffe. He was the acting commander of the 101st Airborne Division when the enemy besieged the division in the Belgian town of Bastonge in the winter of 1944. This became known as the Battle of the Bulge.

The enemy commander offered McAuliffe surrender terms. One of the results of refusing those terms would be a massive artillery bombardment of Bastogne and the surrounding area.

In his exasperation, McAuliffe just said, **AW NUTS!** which became the official response to the enemy.

We are all getting used to a new reality. We are going to get frustrated. Sometimes all we need to do is say, AW NUTS, and drive on.

I come back to Viktor Frankl. We can choose to let our frustrations get the better of us, or we can say, AW NUTS, and drive on.

I am reminded about something Winston Churchill said in December 1940 to the Canadian parliament: "We have not journeyed across the centuries, across the oceans, across the mountains, across the prairies, because we are made of sugar candy."

Enjoy your candy and nuts today.

Eugene

Good afternoon everyone

Today's thought comes from Albert Camus. He said, **Without work, all life goes rotten, but when work is soulless, life stifles and dies.**

Please make sure you take some time each day as you work to find a way to refresh your soul. It could be looking at some art or enjoying some music.

While we are all separated from what is familiar in our respective work lives, the need to find ways to refresh the spirit becomes all the more critical.

Think about the environment of your home workspace. That can be an excellent way to bring life and vitality to your soul, and that vitality may well spill over into your work.

Have a great weekend.

Eugene

Good Morning

Today, you get *two* quotes:

- **The only time to eat diet food is while you are waiting for the steak to cook. – Julia Child**

- **Life is a banquet, and most poor suckers are STARVING to death! – Auntie Mame (as spoken by Rosalind Russell)**

No doubt, we are all eating diet food, metaphorically speaking, since we are all getting used to a whole set of new realities. Even though we are still waiting for the steak to cook, there is no reason for us to starve to death.

Family life, professional life, spiritual life can still be a banquet. We have to get creative about it. The only limitations are the limits of our imagination.

Once we finish with our diet foot, I would submit that the steak that is cooking will have more zest, spice, and flavor.

Enjoy your banquet of life.

Eugene

Good afternoon

Let's all go out to sea!!

- **If the highest aim of a captain were to preserve his ship, he would keep it in port forever. – Thomas Aquinas**

Now, more than ever, we all need the courage to move into deep waters. We need to move into the deep waters personally, professionally, and in our relationships with others.

This courage to move out into the deep is not the exceptional courage of a knight in shining armor ready to do battle. It is the courage of the small hours when decisions to act and how to act are taken, often in quiet and solitude.

But are we all alone as we move into the deep? Many of us are indeed working in isolation, and I would submit to you that you need not move out into the deep alone. We have an opportunity to build a great fleet where all can move forward into the deep together with each other's support.

As the late shipping magnate Aristotle Onassis said, "We must learn to sail in high winds."

Let's all learn how to do that together.

Enjoy your sailing today.

Eugene

# APRIL 2020

# 1 April 2020

Good Morning Everyone

Nobel laureate, diplomat, and civil rights activist Dr. Ralph Bunche said:

- **"Hearts are the strongest when they beat in response to noble ideas."**

Now, I know that we all are focusing on staying productive and helping our respective organizations weather this pandemic.

I would submit that this pandemic might be the catalyst for considering some noble ideas, specifically outreach and building community.

We have the opportunity, and some may say the duty, to reach out to others, be they clients or family members or members of our respective professions. We need to be there for them. Today, you may be the friendly ear that somebody needs, the kind word spoken at precisely the right moment, the smile to somebody at their wit's end. Today, you can be that person because if life teaches us anything, it is that "what goes around, comes around," and tomorrow, you may need the kind word and the smile.

What will be your noble idea today?

Eugene

# 2 April 2020

Good Morning

We've gotten over the "hump" of the week, and some of us (read: me) may be a little tired, so I thought this quote might be something rejuvenating:

- **Wherever there is a human being, there is an opportunity for kindness. – Lucius Annaeus Seneca**

These days, we all (me especially) need to take every opportunity to show kindness, especially given the fact that we might be isolated from others.

Opportunities for kindness will pop up in the most unexpected places. Please seize them!

Enjoy your kindness opportunities!

Eugene

# 3 April 2020

Good afternoon

It's Friday, at the end of a long week. Here is something to take with you through the weekend:

- **Did I offer peace today? Did I bring a smile to someone's face? Did I say words of healing? Did I let go of my anger and resentment? Did I forgive? Did I love? These are the real questions. I must trust that the little bit of love that I sow now will bear many fruits, here in this world and the life to come. – Henri Nouwen**

The weekend can be a time of rest, recreation, and reconnection. Take some time this weekend to bring some peace, a smile, and some healing to a fractious and stressed world, community or household.

I'm sure the seeds of peace you sow this weekend will bear fruit next week.

Have a good weekend.

Eugene

Good Morning

Happy Monday.

We have new week and new opportunities to be a resources for each other.

- **I will give you the best I have – George C. Marshall**

Historians say that one of the reasons General Marshall was not given overall command of the Allies' invasion of Europe during World War II was because FDR said he could not sleep well with General Marshall out of the country.

This week is a new week in our new reality. We all have the opportunity to be of service to each other and to deliver value to our colleagues and clients.

Every day, every encounter with a person is an opportunity to give one's best. It's not easy at times and some days our "best" may not be as "best" as other days.

The key to remember is that we have the opportunity to try; for our families, our co-workers, our clients, and ourselves.

The great coach Vince Lombardi said, "The only place success comes before work is in the dictionary".

United with you in your efforts today and every day!

Eugene

Good Morning

Let's find some joy today.

- **Service which is rendered without joy helps neither the servant nor the served. But all other pleasures and possessions pale into nothingness before service which is rendered in a spirit of joy. – Mahatma Gandhi**

As we go about our daily routines in the new realities of our professional and personal lives – especially given the isolation many of us are working in – I think it is paramount that we find some sort of joy that can accompany our work. Granted, it may be hard to find but I would submit that being able to find some joy, be it the opportunity to see things greening up in the front yard or looking forward to a good meal at the end of the day, can add the needed joy to our daily life.

Maybe the joy can be found in the fact that we may be isolated from each other but in fact, we are all striving in the same direction, namely, to stay safe, healthy, and to help other to do so.

Hoping you find *your* joy today!

Eugene

Good Morning

It looks like resilience and good humor are cut from the same cloth.

- **I grew up a skinny kid with a funny last name and coke bottle glasses, so I experienced my fair share of bullies. But I learned, with the help of humor and resilience, to never give up. – John Hickenlooper**

Every day is a new challenge and a unique opportunity. It seems that it's not enough just to have a stiff upper lip exclusively or just screw on a smile all the time. Both are needed.

Take time today to practice *both* resiliency and good humor to get you through these days. Undoubtedly, in the coming weeks we will need both, so the more we develop them now, the better equipped we will be in the future.

Joining you with good humor and resilience.

Eugene

# 9 April 2020

Good Morning

I'm thinking about creativity this morning. Who would suspect that creativity can flourish in a time of isolation?

- **There are incalculable resources in the human spirit once it has been set free. – Hubert Humphrey**

Maybe this time of isolation is a time for us to look inward, not in a negative way, but in a way that offers a chance to think about the gifts, talents, and skills we bring to everyday life. Sometimes, when we're in a rush, we may forget about what we bring to the table.

I would submit that, possibly, this is a time to assess our gifts and, in a certain way, rejoice in what we have. Our ability to share them, even in these difficult situations, might allow us to recognize others' gifts and skills, and rejoice in them too.

The trick will be to continue to remember and to further develop those gifts when things return to a "new normal."

Rejoicing in your gifts.

Eugene

# 10 April 2020

Good Morning

I have been thinking about light and darkness this morning.

- **Hope is being able to see that there is light despite all of the darkness. – Desmond Tutu**

We've all heard about the eventual light at the end of the tunnel that is this pandemic. Still, I would submit that, while we are in this dark and challenging time, there are lights that act as beacons and provide the needed hope and uplift so that we can continue to do what we must; to support our families, friends, communities, and the other constituencies that we serve. Those lights come to us in thousands of different ways, from the cop on the beat, to the nurse in the hospital, to the grocery store clerk.

If truth be told, each of us, great and small, is a beacon of light and hope for each other.

I don't consider it a coincidence that I am thinking of such things at this time, during the great seasons of Passover and Easter. Please accept my best wishes to you if you are celebrating either one of these great feasts.

Over the past few days, I have seen the forsythia plant in my front yard come into full flower with its yellow flowers. Every day, it is getting brighter and brighter.

Even nature teaches us to hope.

Joining with you in light and hope.

Eugene

# 13 April 2020

Good Morning

- **We must dare to think "unthinkable" thoughts. We must learn to explore all the options and possibilities that confront us in a complex and rapidly changing world. – J. William Fulbright.**

Here we are at the start of a new week: new challenges, new opportunities, new realities.

I'm thinking that most of us have been trying to get used to the "new reality" of things for about three weeks now, and it might be starting to get a little old.

Maybe now is the time to harken back to a time in our lives when things were fresh, new, and unique to capture that sense of creativity and adventure.

I'm a big believer in the law of averages. I may come up with 100 ideas; ninety-nine of them may be total duds, but one idea might be exactly what is needed. If we all take enough chances, sooner or later, the one chance we take will be the one that sets everything in motion.

Joining you in *all* the possibilities

Eugene

# 14 April 2020

Good Morning

- **Iron rusts from disuse; water loses its purity from stagnation ... even so does inaction sap the vigor of the mind. – Leonardo da Vinci**

Teddy Roosevelt was always a proponent of what he called "the strenuous life." TR was referring to a strenuous and active physical life, but I am also sure that he would have advocated for a vigorous and strenuous life of the mind.

Now, more than ever, do we need to stay mentally sharp. I recall watching a documentary on life in wartime Britain and one of the highest-rated radio shows was called *The Brains Trust*, a weekly intellectual panel discussion. This same documentary also talked about people's desire for good music and good art. This phenomenon was found not only in wartime Britain but in Russia as well with the popularity of wartime poets like Konstantin Simonov.

Take time this day or week to do something to renew the vigor of your mind, be it a reading book or listening to music or some writing. I will do the same.

Connecting with you in the life of the mind.

Eugene

Good Morning

- **Nothing in life is to be feared; it is only to be understood. Now is the time to understand more so that we may fear less. – Marie Curie**

No doubt, we are living in a time of great uncertainty. Our physical isolation can take that uncertainty and turn it into fear.

There is no better time than the present to take the strength that lies within each one of us and turn that strength to develop a better understanding of who we are, the people with whom we live and work, and greater society as a whole.

I am convinced that the effort we make now, in this time of uncertainty, will render considerable benefits to us as human beings once this time of uncertainty is over. The ability to be more caring and understanding of each other will shape the world for the better.

Journeying with you on the path of understanding.

Eugene

# 16 April 2020

Good Morning

It's a great morning, and I am feeling optimistic.

- **In its essence, optimism is not a way of looking at the present situation but a power of life, a power of hope when others resign, a power to hold our heads high when all seems to have come to naught, a power to tolerate setbacks, a power that never abandons the future to the opponent but lays claim to it. – Dietrich Bonhoeffer**

Now, this an excellent quote from a German clergyman, but I think it takes on even greater significance when you know the context. Bonhoeffer was part of the 1944 plot to overthrow Hitler. He wrote this while imprisoned by the Nazis. The complete essay can be found here: https://www.intellectualtakeout.org/blog/how-bonhoeffer-dealt-despair-world-chaos/.

It never fails to amaze me how the human spirit, in the face of some very brutal realities, can rise and, as Bonhoeffer states, lay claim to a better future.

In what ways are you laying your claim to a better future?

An esteemed colleague of mine sent around this link. I thought you might enjoy it: https://www.youtube.com/watch?v=tLpihMp1ol8

Joining with you in laying claim to a brighter future.

Eugene

Good Morning Everyone

It's a snowy morning here in Chicago. Will spring ever truly arrive?

It's been a tough week for many. We read in the press of job losses and cutbacks on all fronts, and maybe we are apt to lose faith and hope in each other. Here is something to consider.

- **Hope is like peace. It is not a gift from God. It is a gift only we can give one another. – Elie Wiesel**

We hear a lot about hope and how it comes from within, but Mr. Wiesel turns it on its head. He says that we get hope from each other. Maybe that is the thought for the weekend: that the hope that we carry can be contagious (let's face the facts; we all know a lot more about contagion than we did six weeks ago).

Maybe it's our "duty" (for want of a better word) to carry and express hope, not so much for ourselves, but perhaps for the people we come in contact with. Hope may become the tremendous categorical imperative that

Immanuel Kant speaks about.

Together with you in spreading hope.

Eugene

Good Morning

I read Peggy Noonan's article that appeared in the April 11-12 copy of *The Wall Street Journal*. She interviewed noted social psychologist Jonathan Haidt, and he made the following statement:

- **This is a time for us to reflect and choose a better story. Right now stories are being re-written all around us, nationally, individually, and we all get a chance to do some of the rewriting.**

This reminds me of a line from David Lean's epic film, *Lawrence of Arabia*. The context is different, but the underlying fact is still the same (https://yarn.co/yarn-clip/190a3a6a-95ce-44bb-ac71-f4ae3315ac28).

We can choose to act or be acted upon. This pandemic has sent much of what we know into a tailspin.

We are at the start of a new week. How are we going to change our story this week for the better? How are we going to use this time to make the first rough draft of our new story? No doubt there will be re-writes along the way, but I think the point is that we use this time to make a start and draft a better story for us, our families, the people we work with, and society.

Accompanying you in your writing.

Eugene

Good Morning

Let's all be global do-gooders!

- **I'm convinced of this: Good done anywhere is good done everywhere. For a change, start by speaking to people rather than walking by them like they're stones that don't matter. As long as you're breathing, it's never too late to do some good. – Maya Angelou**

- **Whoever saves one life saves the world entire. – The Talmud**

Isolation, social distancing, masks, contagion – these are the watchwords of our new reality.

I am absolutely convinced that while science will eventually defeat COVID-19, it is the kindness we show each other during this time that will keep that victory from being a hollow one. We need to be more creative in showing compassion: the tap on the window to the neighbor as they pass by, the phone call in the middle of the day to an old friend, the phone call to a business associate to see how they are faring. Maybe even taking pen to paper and actually *writing* a letter!

The more creative we get in showing kindness to each other, the more we can transform the world. That one small act of kindness could impact somebody's life in a large or small way.

With you in saving the world entirely; one kindness at a time.

Eugene

Good Morning

Let's take a walk over to the blacksmith's forge.

- **In this world, a man must either be anvil or hammer – Henry Wadsworth Longfellow. (N.B. I think Goethe also said something like this.)**

When offered this choice, I've heard a lot of people say they would rather be the hammer. The question then is which one gets worn out first?

It goes without saying that this pandemic has been hammering us all in many ways: economically, socially, professionally, and psychologically.

Whether we like it or not, we are all in this together for the long haul. We can let this defeat us, or we can take the appropriate measure to minimize the spread and come out better for it on the other side.

I am absolutely convinced of the fact that we can come out of this as better human beings, and the companies we work for and the associations we are members of will be all the better for it.

A good sense of humor, a sense of proportionality, generosity of spirit on our part, and kindness will wear out that hammer long before the anvil shows signs of wear.

Be strong, be the anvil!

With you in the blacksmith's forge.

Eugene

Good Morning

It looks like I am still in the blacksmith's forge today.

- **Do not wait to strike till the iron is hot; but make it hot by striking. – William Butler Yeats**

Many people are starting to talk about when we get back to "normal" (whatever that is). People are making all sorts of plans of how things will be changed, and they will be better, yadda, yadda, yadda.

I would submit that we need not wait. We don't have to wait until the iron is hot to strike. We all have opportunities right now – both great and small – to strike and forge a new future. Granted, it is easier to form iron when it is hot, but I also would submit to you that it is better to be the one forming the iron from the get-go.

So it is with every facet of our lives. Yes, things are hard now, but I would also submit that now is the time to forge new realities for ourselves in all facets of our lives: personal, professional, familial, and as part of the larger society. We can be leaders in thought (and action) now, as opposed to being the ones who are simply "testing the waters" and "seeing which way the wind is blowing."

Be the blacksmith ... start forging your iron now!

Joining with you at the forge.

Eugene

Good Morning

Well, I finally decided to leave the blacksmith's forge.

- **When you arise in the morning, think of what a precious privilege it is to be alive – to breathe, to think, to enjoy, to love. – Marcus Aurelius**

Not all of us are morning people. Some need that first cup of coffee or tea to get them started. Others might want a nice hot (or cold) shower.

Maybe, no matter what we use to start our day, if we have this as our first thought it might set the tenor for the rest of the day.

It's been said that it takes twenty-eight consecutive days of doing something before it becomes a habit. I would submit to you that this thought might be a habit worth starting.

During this time of pandemic and uncertainty, we will have good days and bad days. Having this thought rattling around in our minds might take the edge off the bad days.

No doubt, there are folks better off and worse off than us during this pandemic, but I'm not sure that such comparisons are helpful. We have an opportunity to really look and realize what a privilege it is to get up in the morning and let that realization spill over into all the interactions we have in the day.

Have a great weekend!

Journeying with you in the privilege of life.

Eugene

Good Morning

We are at the start of a new week. I've heard many people say that things are starting to feel like the movie *Groundhog Day*, the same thing every day. Here is something that Justice Holmes once said that might help counter that:

- **Life is painting a picture, not doing a sum. – Oliver Wendell Holmes, Jr.**

Each day, each week, gives us the opportunity to add something to the painting that is our life. Sometimes the things we add to that painting are small details, sometimes they are massive statements, but all go into making up the art that is our lives.

Not only can we add to our painting, but we have the opportunity to add to the paintings of those around us: our family, work colleagues, clients, and maybe even the people we see passing in front of our homes.

Take those opportunities as they arise. Make a difference. Add a splash of color to somebody's painting and let somebody add a splash of color to yours.

Partnering with you at the easel.

Eugene

Good Morning

It's been said that there is a difference between existing and truly living.

- **My mission in life is not merely to survive but to thrive; and to do so with some passion, some compassion, some humor, and some style. – Maya Angelou**

We've all heard about the need for compassion and good humor during this COVID-19 crisis, but I think Ms. Angelou is on to something when she says we need some style to thrive.

It can become relatively easy to simply drag yourself out of bed, go to your workspace and grind out another eight hours, but maybe as we work and get through the day, there are little things we can do to exhibit some style. Maybe wear a brightly-colored shirt or scarf. I know of a librarian colleague who wears a different bowtie every day, even though he works from home. Try lighting a candle in your workspace. Stream some good music while you are working.

All these little things can help brighten the day; they don't simply enable us to survive but help us to *really* thrive.

Partnering with you in finding some style and pizazz.

Eugene

Good Morning

Last week I spent some time at the blacksmith's forge.  Today I am in the sculptor's studio.

- **Every block of stone has a statue inside it, and it is the task of the sculptor to discover it. – Michelangelo**

Michelangelo makes an interesting statement.  It seems to me that, to him, the form, or the finished statue, lies not only in the mind and vision of the sculptor but also as a physical reality within the block of stone, and those two equally valid realities are what makes something beautiful.

Can it also be said of our future?  It is the work that we do now that will determine our future.  Every time we reach out to family, friends, colleagues, clients, or even strangers in the street, we are in some incalculable way striking the hammer and chisel on the stone and helping to bring forth a future.

Sometimes our vision of the future is obscured, sometimes we don't seem to be making a lot of progress in the carving, but I am convinced that the continued efforts at carving will reveal good things in the future.

Extending the sculpture analogy a little further, we must keep our tools sharp during the carving.  You will know that Covey calls this "sharpening the saw" for those of you who have experience with Covey training.  Take time to read, learn and expand your intellectual vistas.

United with you in the carving.

Eugene

Good Morning

Most of us are pretty homebound right now, so let's think about doing some traveling.

- **Two roads diverged in a wood and I took the one less traveled by, and that has made all the difference. – Robert Frost**

It sounds pretty odd to be thinking about traveling while most everything is at a standstill in that respect. Or is it?

Upon the first glance, it could be that Frost is talking about an actual physical journey. Let's look at this in the context of a different type of trip.

This pandemic has forced us all on a different road. A road not only less traveled but one that we are all cutting out of a wilderness. This cutting will be, and has been, long and hard, and it's not without its setbacks.

That being said, a very dismal conclusion could be drawn, but I reject that. I am convinced that this road we are collectively building will lead to something good inside each one of us. This will be something that each person must find in the solitude of their own heart and spirit, and it is up to each one of us to decide how that good thing is going to be used for the benefit of the people around us: family, friends, co-workers, clients, and the society as a whole.

Together with you on the road less traveled.

Eugene

# MAY 2020

# 1 May 2020

Good Morning

Today's quote comes from my friend Steve Wasserman from the west coast (thank you very much, Steve).

- **There are two paths you can go by, but in the long run, there's still time to change the road you're on – Led Zepplin**

No doubt, the past month and a half has forced us to change the road we are on. The question is, are we stuck on that road?

Now, I am in no way advocating actions that would endanger personal or community health and safety. What I am saying is that, even as we move along this road, we can change it. We can change it by our actions towards each other and by our attitudes. Some may see this time as an adventure; some may see it as a time for reflection; some may see this as a time for reconnection; all these perspectives are, in essence, changing the road that one is on.

Not only can we change the road that we are on, but by our actions, we can influence the road that others are on for the better. Every time we reach out to a family member, friend, colleague, or client, we can make the journey on their road easier in some incalculable way.

Have a great weekend.

Your traveling companion.

Eugene

Good Morning

Here we are at the start of a new week. I hope everyone was able to enjoy the weekend.

- **The most important thing is to try and inspire people so that they can be great in whatever they want to do. – Kobe Bryant**

We are living in strange and challenging times. The tendency in human nature is to try and run to security during times of peril or uncertainty. Now, more than ever, we need to find something within ourselves that will not only inspire others but inspire ourselves. That inspiration can be the fuel that will see us through this difficult time.

Every encounter we have with others is an opportunity to inspire. Actions small and great can provide that much-needed spark. The novelty of sheltering in place/working from home has worn off for many of us. Now is the time to take what we have inside and use it to inspire ourselves to excellence. That inspirational force is different for every person. We owe it to ourselves, our families, the people we work with, and humanity as a whole to grab hold of it. We will all be better off for it.

Seeking inspiration with you this week.

Eugene

5 May 2020

Good Morning

I went out this morning to do some shopping, and it put me in the mood to think about where I am going.

- **Consider your origins: you were not made to live as brutes, but to follow virtue and knowledge. – Dante Alighieri**

This continued isolation can sometimes lead many (read: me) to forget who they are and focus simply on survival. I believe that, even in isolation and uncertainty, we can still follow and seek virtue and knowledge. Every day, we have a chance to choose how we are going to approach that day. We can choose to practice virtue in many different manifestations; we can do small kindnesses to the people we live with, we can reach out to somebody who may need a smile or a kind word or just a little bit more patience.

We also can choose to expand our knowledge. Be it in some small way that helps us through the day (or maybe the next five minutes) or larger ways to help the people we work with, our families, or clients.

It goes without saying that some days, it will be harder to follow virtue and knowledge than others. Take the risk: seek virtue and knowledge and remember the common humanity that binds us all together.

United with you in the search for virtue and knowledge.

Eugene

Good Morning Everyone

Welcome to Wednesday (aka Hump Day)

- **A good laugh is sunshine in the house. – William Makepeace Thackeray**

It's been said that laughter is the best medicine, which is a treatment we need now more than ever. I'm not talking about the polite chuckle here or there but a knockdown, drag-out laugh that takes you a good half-hour to get over. When was the last time any of us got really silly and invoked such a laugh in others or ourselves?

In the Bible, the Book of *Ecclesiastes* says that there is a time to weep and a time to laugh. Maybe there should be some time in every day to laugh.

If we lose our sense of humor and sense of fun during this pandemic, I think we will have lost something fundamental; something that can make us more human, more caring, and more compassionate.

I know that sometimes I get the biggest laughs from my own follies.

Take the opportunity today and every day to find some humor.

Laughing with you today and every day.

Eugene

Good Morning

Do you remember your multiplication tables?

- **Perpetual optimism is a force multiplier. – Colin Powel**

In military science, force multiplication or a force multiplier refers to a factor or a combination of factors that gives personnel or weapons (or other hardware) the ability to accomplish greater feats than without it.

We all need our force multipliers, now more than ever. Anything that you can draw on to give you that little burst of energy at the end of a long day, or help keep you focused when distractions abound, are your force multipliers.

I would submit to you that we can be each other's force multiplier. We are indeed separated by distance, but we have the means to be that resource, that kind word, that concerned outreach that will help sustain others and sustain ourselves.

But that's not the whole of it. We are not meant to simply sustain. We are meant to flourish. Being a force multiplier can become a habit, and therein lies the key to flourishing. I am convinced that the support, care, and concern we show now will come back to each of us in abundance.

No doubt being a force multiplier engenders some risk. There is always the risk that you will be rejected. In this pandemic, the easy thing to do is to run to safety and not reach out, but isn't the one of the purposes of life itself to reach out, show compassion, and be that force multiplier for others? Advancing with you as the force multiplier.

Eugene

Good Morning

We've come to the end of another week of sheltering in place, so maybe it's a good time to think about where you live.

- **I dwell in possibility. – Emily Dickinson**

I don't think Ms. Dickinson is talking about where we make our physical abode (the place where the mail gets delivered), but I think she is talking about a mindset. Interestingly, she uses the word "dwell". That word conjures up images of home; a place of permanence, not something transient. To dwell in possibility means that the idea of things being possible is an ever-present, abiding perspective and attitude.

Today we celebrate V-E Day's 75th anniversary, which brought the Second World War in Europe to an end. No doubt that, from the highest echelon of command to the common soldier, sailor, or airman, they all had to dwell in possibility, or they would not have been able to bring about so great a victory.

We all must dwell in possibility; the possibility that this pandemic will end, the possibility that we will emerge from it better people, and the possibility that society as a whole will be better. Without dwelling in possibility, we might as well shelter in place forever.

Maybe part of what we need to do is bring more people into the "dwelling" of possibility. Family, friends, co-workers, clients, everyone we meet.

Dwelling with you in possibility.

Eugene

Good Morning

It's a grey Monday here in Chicago, and it's put me in the mood to think about getting up and getting on with it (whatever that is).

- **You are not going to be perfect every day. It's about turning up the next day and doing it again. – Krista Tippet**

We are at the start of a new week, with new challenges and new opportunities. Sometimes it's hard to capitalize on those challenges and opportunities and think with the end in mind.

In those cases, maybe the victory merely is getting up, getting dressed, and getting on with the day.

I remember reading somewhere that the famous social activist Monsignor Jack Egan was talking to a fellow priest who was older and ailing. This more senior priest was looking back on his priesthood with some disappointment. Egan told this priest that, at the least, he showed up.

That "showing up" every day, consistently, and being present to our families, friends, co-workers, and clients is what's going to lead us through this pandemic and to a better day.

We are not guaranteed any modicum of success in our endeavors, but I am sure that there will be no success without that first step, and that is to show up.

Partnering with you in showing up today.

Eugene

Good Morning

An old saying goes something like this: tell me who your friends are, and I will tell you what you are like.

- **Look at people for an example, but then make sure to do things your way. Surround yourself with positive people. – Queen Latifah**

I think now, more than ever, it is vital that we surround ourselves with people who have a natural, positive energy. Let's face it, we all have our bad days when the positive energy is at a low ebb. It's at those times that the positive influence of others can be so significant.

Now, during this time of sheltering in place, it may be harder to connect with those we can draw that positive energy. Make an effort; make that phone call, open the door, call out and greet a neighbor, and write that letter.

Your simple act may be the catalyst that will start somebody else's positive energy and outlook.

Sharing the positive energy with you.

Eugene

Good Morning

Happy Wednesday to you.  Did you make your bed today?

- **If you want to change the world, start off by making your bed.
– William H. McRaven**

Admiral McRaven wrote a book based on this principle.  I think he is saying that doing the little things early in the day can set a tenor and tone for the rest of the day.  I know from personal experience that if I go to my bedroom in the evening and see an unmade bed, I feel a little deflated, no matter what has happened that day.  I think McRaven is also saying that changes and successes build on themselves.  The more changes and successes you accumulate in the course of a day, the more likely you will change the world, or at least change that little part you exist in.

Starting the day with a small accomplishment can lead to bigger things.  In a similar vein, if the day turns out to be a total washout, you can at least say you made your bed.

Small morning rituals like this are so crucial in the times we are living now.  Turn those small rituals into something that can benefit others, especially those with whom you are sheltering in place.

Together with you in changing the world … one made bed at a time.

Eugene

Good Morning

Happy Friday! I hope everyone finds sometime this week to recharge, renew and reconnect.

I've been thinking about the nature of work.

- **Work to me is a sacred thing. – Margaret Bourke-White**

I remember somebody interviewing Ms. Bourke-White. This person asked Ms. Bourke-White how she could get her subjects to work so hard during a photoshoot. Bourke-White responded that she could get her subject to work hard because they saw how hard she was working.

We have examples every day of people working hard around us: the medical professionals, the cop on the beat, the harried store clerk, the bleary-eyed truck driver. All these are examples of people putting in hard work.

When I speak of work, I am not only referring to those activities for which we receive a monetary wage. It also includes the work and effort we put in to make our homes a place of joy and refuge during this trying time. The effort we put in to make the lives of others a little easier is also work. Finally, the work we put in to make ourselves better human beings. All these things are work, and all of them are sacred and transcendent, and transformational.

Your work, your effort, can change the world.

Laboring with you in the sacred.

Eugene

Good Morning

Happy Monday and the start of a new week.

- **One thing I know: the only ones among you who will be really happy are those who will have sought and found how to serve. – Albert Schweitzer**

What I find interesting in Dr. Schweitzer's words is that one has to seek and discover how to serve. It's not something innate in human nature. I may take issue with Dr. Schweitzer's words because I think we all want to be useful and helpful, but maybe that is the optimist in me coming out.

Maybe what we need to seek and find are the ways we express our desire to be useful. How are we responding to that voice inside each of us that calls us to the service to others? Some may simply choose to ignore that voice, and others may have other voices that drown it out.

I have learned from people in AA and other twelve-step programs that sobriety is achieved one day at a time. Maybe it is the same for being of service; one just needs to respond to the call of service today.

In this pandemic, the opportunities to be of service in large and small ways are as numerous as the sands of the seashore. The key is to find that grain of sand and make it your own. Do that enough times, and you will wind up with a beautiful beach. In some way, your service may help create a beautiful beach for somebody else, be they a family member, work colleague, or client. The key is to reach out and make an effort.

With you in beach building.

Eugene

Good Morning

I was thinking … we have spent time at the blacksmith's forge, in the sculptor's studio, and today we are doing some carpentry.

- **If opportunity doesn't knock, build a door. – Milton Berle**

It's easy to only think of Mr. Berle dressed up in a dress or doing the "Uncle Milty" routine from the golden age of television, but I think he has some wisdom for us today.

It's been said that one makes their own breaks; nothing of value is really handed to a person, which is indeed true. Opportunities come, by and large, through effort.

What I want to consider, though, is what happens after the door is built. Do we brick it up and force the next person to bust through and build it again from scratch, or do we put up a big "Open!" sign and a lighted path for others to follow?

There is an old adage in the world of carpentry: "Measure twice, cut once." Maybe all that attention to detail is not meant just for us, but for those who come after us.

During this time of pandemic and sheltering in place, it can be easy to turn inward. Maybe this is time to reach out to others and help them with their measuring and cutting as they build their doors, and likewise, we should welcome those who want to join us in building our doors.

Our friends, family members, co-workers, clients, and people we pass in the street are building a myriad of doors to uncover countless opportunities that we can take part in, both now and when this pandemic is over.

It's just a case of us showing up with our tape measure, hammer, and a box of nails.

On a side note: Please be careful and don't mash your thumb with your hammer.

Laboring with you in the carpenter's shop.

Eugene

Good Morning

It's a beautiful morning here in Chicago, so there's no better time to bring up a *very* popular subject … Rent.

- **Service is the rent that you pay for room on this earth. – Shirley Chisholm**

There is an old saying about folks who buy houses that goes something like this: you pay rent to a landlord, and at the end of the year, all you have are rent receipts.

Whether we like it or not, we are all accumulating some rent receipts for our room on this earth. The question is, what is written on those receipts? Are things like kindness, compassion, inclusion, diligence, collaboration, or a myriad of other virtues being written down?

We all collect rent receipts in this life, some good, some not so good. Maybe the key is to try and minimize the bad receipts and maximize the good ones.

We are regularly presented with opportunities to fill our life's rent receipt book. Unlike rent paid on an apartment, the amount of each of life's rent receipts can be vastly different amounts, and it is often the receipts for the smaller payments that can make such a difference, not only in our lives, but in the lives of others.

The beauty of life's rent receipt book is that filling it up is not contingent on the size of one's bank account, the level of one's education, birth, or upbringing. What fills up the receipt book comes from deep inside a person and is made manifest by their choices.

What sort of rent receipts will you be writing today?

Together with you in paying life's rent.

Eugene

Good Morning

Maybe it's good to think about creativity as we head into a long weekend.

- **I'm always thinking about creating. My future starts when I wake up every morning … Every day I find something creative to do with my life. – Miles Davis**

It's interesting to note that Mr. Davis seems to always have creativity at the forefront of his thoughts. It could be argued that it becomes his energy for the day. The alternative to creative energy for the day is one that reflects only survival. How many times have we all said to ourselves something akin to, "If I can just get through the day." I know I have done it, and that can drain creative energy faster than anything else.

So, what is the alternative? What can one do to help reignite the creative spirit?

First off, be sure you are taking care of yourself. Eat well, get plenty of sleep, and some exercise, both physical and spiritual.

Next, maybe it is advisable to try something a little out of the ordinary. We have this long weekend coming up. Perhaps it is a ripe opportunity to try something different, be it a new recipe or planting something different in the garden or maybe reaching out to people who are not in your immediate circle. Perhaps it's time to make a new friend, even in this time of social distancing and sheltering in place.

Maybe a new experience is just what we all sometimes need to knock creativity from the back of the mind to the front of the mind.

Basking with you in the creative forces.

Eugene

Good Morning

We're at the beginning of a long weekend, but as we relax and recharge, we are still called to act.

- **To love is to act. – Victor Hugo**

These words were the last words in Mr. Hugo's diary, written two weeks before his death.

If we expand the meaning of love, not just to mean romantic love but care, concern and empathy, I think Mr. Hugo is trying to say that it's not enough to only speak of these things. To manifest them, one must act on them.

It is a good and noble thing to plan our acts of charity and care, but it is also vital that we act upon those charitable and care-filled instincts that surprise us. Those spontaneous acts could very well be an expression of the most profound feelings in the human soul: the desire to be connected with others.

We have a long weekend coming. This can and should be a time for relaxation and rejuvenation, but it can also be a time in the quiet to listen to the calling of the inner voice which longs for connection. Make some phone calls this weekend, write a letter, wave to the neighbors.

Dr. Martin Luther King said, "**We must learn to live together as brothers or perish together as fools.**"

Joined with you in not being a fool.

Eugene

Good Evening

We are coming to the end of the Memorial Day holiday. I can remember when people called it Decoration Day.

- **True patriotism isn't cheap. It's about taking on a fair share of the burden of keeping America going. – Robert Reich**

I have had the honor several times of walking through the grounds and lanes of Arlington National Cemetery. The rows of neatly arranged white headstones, brilliant in the summer sun, give silent and poignant witness to what love of country means.

Frequently, when people talk about "fair share" and "burden," some will interpret it to mean taxes. I would submit that the fair share of the burden includes compassion, inclusion, optimism, and hard work. All these attributes are part and parcel of the burden of keeping America going.

This pandemic calls upon us all to draw from our interior well of goodness, compassion, optimism, and hard work. It takes courage and determination to draw from that well. It is easy not to draw from that well and let the other person do it.

Each person drawing from their well of compassion and care will cause a great draught that will change individuals, neighborhoods, cities, and the world at large.

What will you bring out from your well today?

Joined with you at the well.

Eugene

Good Morning

Here we are, at the start of another work week, albeit a shortened one. Weather-wise, we have moved from having to run the furnace last Friday to starting up the air conditioner last night. I guess we have moved into a new season, no matter what the calendar says. Maybe in this new season, it might be worth thinking about creativity for a moment.

- **Creativity takes courage. – Henri Matisse**

Now more than ever, we need to think and act creatively. We need to be creative in our approach to life and relationships. Especially now, while people are sheltering in place, we need to find creative ways of staying connected as family, colleagues, and a society. As we endeavor to shape our new world creatively, it will take courage: courage over the fear of failure, courage over the cynicism of others, and courage over the fear of rejection as we reach out to others.

It took courage for Matisse to bring forth his creative art style. It will take courage from us to create a better world after this pandemic.

Take a chance ... be courageous ... be creative.

Partnering with you in courage and creativity.

Eugene

Good Morning

With the coming of summer, the days are getting longer, and we have more daylight.

- **There are two ways of spreading light: to be the candle or the mirror that reflects it. – Edith Wharton**

Everyone has a role to play in helping us get through this pandemic. Some make things happen, and some use the tools they have to reflect the goodness being created by others. Both are equally important and necessary. The more opportunities to make connections between people, to show compassion, to create meaning, the more there is for others to reflect, both in their own lives and to others' lives.

We can't all be present in all places and be all things to all people, but we can catch that spark, that light of goodness and compassion, and reflect it in the lives of others.

What light will you be creating and reflecting today?

With you in kindling and reflecting light.

Eugene

Good Morning

Let's all go to the theater this morning.

- **Life's like a play: it's not the length, but the excellence of the acting that matters. – Lucius Annaeus Seneca**

Right now, we are all playing a part in a very interesting play. Who would have thought six months ago that the play we were in, the script, the staging, and the players, would all be radically changed?

The question now is, how are we going act in this new play? Some of us have large roles, some have small roles, some have roles that are always changing.

At the end of this play, what will the reviews be? No matter what the role, script, or staging, we can all play the parts we have been given with a sense of grace, charity, thoughtfulness, and kindness. In the final analysis, isn't that how we would want our performance to be reviewed?

Let this time of pandemic and sheltering in place be a time that brings out the best performance in all of us.

Supporting you in the theater of life.

Eugene

Good Morning

It's a beautiful spring morning with lots of potential.  Why not enjoy it?

- **Others have seen what is and asked why. I have seen what could be and asked why not. – Pablo Picasso**

This pandemic has undoubtedly caused many of us to ask the "why" questions: why now? why me? why my family?  The questions are valid and deserve a proper answer, but my thinking is taking me beyond the "why" to the "why not" that Picasso speaks about.

Each one of us has the potential to take what we have now and turn it into something better.  It's just a case of figuring out what that better thing or situation is.  It doesn't have to be a big thing.  It could be the extra minute we take to look at something outside the window or the opportunity we capitalize on to reach out in kindness and solidarity to another person.

I am convinced that the more we capitalize on the opportunities to create a vision, even a small one, for ourselves and say, "why not," the better we will become as people and as a society as a whole.

The "why not" opportunities are only bounded by our creativity.  We can also latch on to somebody else's "why not" opportunity.  Maybe that's the more urgent thing to do in these difficult times.

What "why not" opportunity will you take a chance on today?

Partnering with you in finding the "why not".

Eugene

Good Afternoon

I usually don't send these messages out on the weekend, but today, I am bound in conscience because of the past few days' events to say something.

- **Because I remember, I despair. Because I remember, I have the duty to reject despair. – Elie Wiesel**

What started as a just and righteous expression of frustration, anger, grief, and mourning of the extrajudicial killing of Mr. Floyd was exploited by some and turned into a night of arson, looting, rioting, and mayhem. These people of violence do not well serve Mr. Floyd's memory.

This has given me pause to consider memories: what we remember, what we forget, and how we respond to what we choose to remember. Some will simply want to forget all these events. I am not sure this is helpful because, if we forget history's lessons, we are doomed to repeat them. Some will want to remember but then respond to those memories with more bitterness, anger, and despair. I don't think that will get us anywhere either.

I think Mr. Wiesel gives us a third way. He is calling us to remember but to use those memories as a catalyst to change our attitude and engender hope. He may be calling us to use these memories: to find somewhere deep inside each of us and to call upon what Lincoln referred to as the better angels of our nature. This task is not without risk and pain and cannot be accomplished without effort and recognition of others' good will.

No one person can change years of negative personal and institutional attitudes. We can, though, make small changes in the orbit in which we have some influence.

Maybe a lesson from nature may be helpful. Diamonds are made up of carbon atoms. It takes only one atom of some other element wedged in the structure of those millions of carbon atoms in that diamond to give it a different, and often, more rare color.

Maybe we are called to be that one atom that adds color and more extraordinary brilliance to life.

Laboring with you in changing the color of diamonds.

Eugene

# JUNE 2020

Good Morning

It is the start of a new work-week at the end of some very tough days and tense nights. Some may look upon this time as our society's dark night of the soul.

- **We draw our strength from the very despair in which we have been forced to live. We shall endure. – Cesar Chavez**

Mr. Chavez offers us a stark and powerful choice. We can either surrender to the despair and desolation surrounding us or harness it to build a better tomorrow. We can retreat into factions, tribes, and interest groups or realize that we are all in this together; we all must endure together and conquer together.

Mr. Chavez makes a definitive statement. We *shall* endure. Not we *might* endure, or we'll endure if we are lucky enough. He says we *will* endure. The choice for us now is how we are going to come out of that endurance. Are we going to come out a broke, hollowed-out people, or will we come out with a newfound sense of each person's dignity and value, each person's strength which has been forged in the crucible of pandemic, injustice, and mayhem in our streets?

I have no easy answers for anyone. I have always been suspicious of those who wish to offer easy answers to tough questions. The bottom line is that we can't win this fight we are in now, if we can't take it.

Amid our endurance, there are both large and small opportunities to strike a blow for our common humanity and a better tomorrow. Every time we reach out to somebody in kindness, concern, and solidarity, we are striking a blow. Every time we put ourselves to the task at hand, either professionally or personally, we are striking a blow to make a better tomorrow.

As I am writing this, I have a growing feeling of militancy. A militancy that is not calling me to violence but a militancy calling me to bind myself ever more closely to my fellow human beings, their innate dignity and value.

Struggling with you in the crucible.

Eugene

Good Morning

It's Tuesday morning, and we are greeted with the news of another night of unrest.

- **History, despite its wrenching pain, cannot be unlived, but if faced with courage, need not be lived again. – Maya Angelou**

No doubt, what we are living through right now is unbelievably wrenching. Like a wrench on a bolt, it twists and turns, causing great agony, distress, and hopelessness. It makes us double over and bow our heads.

But in all that, Ms. Angelou provides words of hope. First off, she calls us to face it. That means we stand erect and turn towards the pain. We cannot run away. She also encourages us to face it *with courage*.

How do we manifest that courage? There is no doubt that there are deep-seated political, social and economic institutions that need to be changed so that each person's inherent dignity and value is not just acknowledged in some superficial way but indeed affirmed and celebrated.

Where do we start? We start as we do all things: by reaching out to other humans in solidarity, care, compassion, and realizing that we are all in this together, whether we live on the same street or the other side of the globe.

The question for each of us is how will we do that outreach *today*? We cannot cry over yesterday's missed opportunities, and we cannot predict what tomorrow will bring. All we can do is capitalize on those opportunities *today*, and maybe not the whole day, but maybe in the next hour or so.

This outreach comes without risk, as with anything worth doing. There is the risk of failure, rejection, and being accused of having mixed motives.

Reach out anyway.  It doesn't have to be a big expressive way.  Often, the smallest acts by many people can make the most significant difference.

Facing the future with you in courage.

Eugene

Good Morning

There has been a good deal of talk recently about being safe. How do we truly achieve that?

- **Where justice is denied, where poverty is enforced, where ignorance prevails, and where any one class is made to feel that society is an organized conspiracy to oppress, rob and degrade them, neither persons nor property will be safe. – Frederick Douglass**

The past week's events have shown that there is still much work to be done in this great American experiment. The job is indeed unfinished, but not impossible.

Some may see these events and despair. I choose not to. I am convinced that, more often than not, bad outcomes are a result of poor systems and flawed processes and not from bad people. It is up to all of us to find ways to change society's systems and processes so that, in the long run, we can achieve what Mr. Douglass is referring to: true safety.

Systems and processes change by improvements, both great and small. We can all do something. Reaching out in solidarity to others to break cycles of isolation is an excellent way to start.

Take some time, now, this day, this week, to reach out to somebody. You don't have to solve their problems. You just need to reach out in solidarity and compassion.

That's a start. Making that start may help stir the internal changes we all must make to help build a truly just, compassionate, and inclusive society.

Laboring with you in finding security.

Eugene

Good Morning

It's a bright new morning, replete with all the potential that it brings.

- **Yesterday is not ours to recover, but tomorrow is ours to win or lose. – Lyndon Johnson**

The verdict of history on Lyndon Johnson is mixed. Today is not the time or place to debate that legacy. I was thinking about President Johnson's very famous picture, where he is seen listening to a tape recording made by his son-in-law Charles Robb, a serving Marine in Vietnam. You can find the image here: https://www.archives.gov/historical-docs/todays-doc/?dod-date=731. The look of pain and anguish in President Johnson is unmistakable.

I wonder what the verdict of history will be on the times we are living in now? What recordings, writings, and other ephemera will people look at, and grieve and mourn over?

Anger, grief, and mourning are all appropriate feelings, but what will win our todays and tomorrows? Nothing can change yesterday: not the violence or injustice wrought, not the pain and loss.

What we can do is look into ourselves; to the store of wealth, strength, and goodness that lies within each one of us, in order to reach out in solidarity, inclusion, with the realization that our common humanity can shape a future that is worthy of our dignity as human beings.

The smallest of gestures today will reap a rich harvest tomorrow.

Joined with you in winning tomorrow's victories.

Eugene

# 5 June 2020

Good Morning

For the past few days, and maybe even for the entire time I have been putting out these messages, I have stressed the importance of reaching out in solidarity to others. Perhaps as the weekend approaches, we need to think about being on the receiving end of that outreach, because let's face it … why should you have all the fun and do all the outreach?

- **You're imperfect, and you're wired for struggle, but you are worthy of love and belonging. – Brene Brown**

Interestingly, Ms. Brown begins with the often uncomfortable fact that we are imperfect but suggests that perhaps out of that imperfection comes the drive to struggle, to try, to reach out. Sometimes (read I), we get so focused on the struggle that we fail to realize that each of us, because of our imperfections, need the care, outreach, and solidarity of others. This care and concern from others is not some quid pro quo; people are only kind to us because we are kind. No, the care and concern of others is our birthright. Whether or not people choose to show that care and concern is another thing.

The fact that we can acknowledge others' worth makes the care we show something beyond mere charity. It is standing in solidarity with them as members of the same human family. When we acknowledge ourselves as worthy of love and belonging and accept acts of care from others, we are also standing in solidarity with them.

So, this weekend, please take some time to be quiet, read something, listen to some good music and allow others to care and stand in solidarity with you. Grateful for the care and concern you show me.

Eugene

Good Morning

It's Monday, and it's another opportunity to do something new.

- **We are here to make another world. – W. Edwards Deming**

Interestingly, Mr. Deming would say we are here to make a *new* world since he was the father of continuous improvement. It seems that Mr. Deming is calling for us to scrap everything and start from scratch … or is he?

The essence of continuous improvement is that you look for where processes are not working, change the process and provide education on those processes.

Our society is replete with processes that are not working. These processes that are not working are costing people their lives. It's not enough for us to say that this-or-that in society is broken. It is incumbent upon us to understand *why* they are broken; how did we get to the state we are in. That is going to involve conversations around race, opportunity, and inclusion. Some people (read: me) may not be comfortable with those conversations. It may require taking a hard look at attitudes we have held for a long time.

We have to be willing to take a chance to have the uncomfortable conversations. If we are willing to do that, we can make a new world that is diverse, inclusive, and healthy for everyone. It means reaching out to others. It means being vulnerable. Take the risk. A new world is depending on it.

Joined with you in the uncomfortable conversation.

Eugene

Good Morning

What do you consider ordinary? What do you consider extraordinary?

- **Your ordinary acts of love and hope point to the extraordinary promise that every human life is of inestimable value. – Desmond Tutu**

What is fascinating to me about what Bishop Tutu has said that it emphasizes that the ordinary, everyday, what some might call run-of-the-mill, acts that lead to something extraordinary.

Each day, we have new opportunities to show ordinary acts of love, hope, care, concern, and solidarity. The bottle of water left for the mailman or the person cutting your lawn on a hot day, the kind word to a spouse, the impromptu call to a friend; all these acts lead to Bishop Tutu's conclusion that every human life is of great value.

Now more than ever, we need to make those small acts of love and care. They need not be announced with a banging drum or tinkling cymbal. All that is necessary is that they be done.

Risk is always an element when one is vulnerable enough to show care and concern. Acts can be misunderstood, motives question, but in the final analysis, it is usually better to take the risk than not.

Maybe it's time we starting thinking and acting honestly about what kind of a block, neighborhood, or city we want to live in.

I am convinced that the accumulation of ordinary acts of love and concern will lead us into a new society of broad, sunlit uplands (to borrow a phrase from Winston Churchill). Now more than ever, we need to develop a vision of a truly just and inclusive society.

That society won't be built on its own. It will be built on the love and concern of others. There will be advances, and there will be setbacks, but the end state is worth the effort.

Joined with you in ordinary acts of love and hope.

Eugene

Good Morning

Who are you? It's a question with infinite possibilities.

- **Never be bullied into silence. Never allow yourself to be made a victim. Accept no one's definition of your life; define yourself. – Harvey Fierstein**

There is so much to unpack here. In this time of pandemic and social unrest (and hopefully positive social change), we are faced with both opportunity and caution. It would be so easy to let current events shape us and define who we are. The stronger thing to do is look at current events and say: How can I redefine myself, my attitudes, and beliefs? Many of us (read: me) are going through that challenging introspection.

To say that things are the way they are and won't change until something else changes, I think, creates a state of perpetual victimhood. I reject that. I think we should be taking up the challenges of recent events to redefine ourselves for the better. I am not calling for some sort of superficial change but a change on a deeper, more substantial level. In ways great and small, we can be the change agents for a new society.

There will be naysayers. There will be people who are telling you that you are wasting your time. Please politely tell them to go pound sand.

It's only through that sort of change will we be able to create a more just, more inclusive, and safer society for all. Anything less is just window dressing.

This change and introspection need not occur alone. To be honest, we probably would be better off if we entered into all sorts of dialog about this. Those dialogs will be uncomfortable at times, but it is the only way forward that I can see.

On the journey with you in redefinition.

Eugene

Good Morning

I was in the Walgreens yesterday and saw a young person walk in with the phrase FINISH ON EMPTY on her jersey, and it made me think of this quote.

- **When I stand before God at the end of my life, I would hope that I would not have a single bit of talent left, and could say, 'I used everything you gave me.' – Erma Bombeck**

The times we are living in are demanding much of everyone. We are being forced into a new way of living and working, and recent events are forcing us to deal, in a realistic and meaningful manner, with issues of race, injustice, equity, and inclusion. These challenges will require the very best of us all and every bit of talent that we can muster.

I have always been a big believer that the whole is always greater than the sum of its parts. Each one of us has some talent, some gift that will help us build a more just, more inclusive society when brought to the fore. This work cannot, and will not, be done in isolation. It will be accomplished only when we all understand the challenge that faces us as a society and the equal and maybe more pointed realization of what will happen if we fail in this great task.

The tasks ahead are not easy, and there will be setbacks. I genuinely believe that it is incumbent on all of us to bring the gifts and talents we all possess to the significant tasks that lie ahead of us.

Some may ask if we as a society are up to the task. I am sorry to say that whether we are up to the job is not the question. The job is there to be done because the alternative is too horrible to contemplate.

Come forward … bring your talents … help create a new society.

Together with you in finishing on empty.

Eugene

Good Morning

Happy Friday, everyone. It's Friday, and with the coming weekend, you know what that means … gardening.

- **Let us be grateful to people who make us happy, they are the charming gardeners who make our souls blossom. – Marcel Proust**

It goes without saying that we are in some tough times, and it is so easy to forget, in our isolation, that each of us has the power to impact so many people (both positively and negatively). Proust reminds us to be grateful for those people that bring happiness into our lives. The corollary to that is part of our gratitude should be to make somebody else happy.

The garden analogy is also helpful because, in order to make a beautiful and healthy garden, it takes all manner of skills. Some people are good at design, some are good at understanding what plants grow best in what location, some are good at garden maintenance. Similarly, each of us has gifts and skills that we can use to make somebody else happy, such as writing a thoughtful note, the ability to bake a pie (yum), the ability to be patient and silent, and simply be present to another person.

More than ever, we need to find those things within ourselves that we can use for the happiness and betterment of those around us. I am convinced that individual isolation is no longer a just or moral action to take. We must reach out with what we have inside to make a better, just, and more inclusive world.

Together with you in working in the garden.

Eugene

Good Morning

Is life sometimes (maybe all the time) like an orchard?

- **You've got to go out on a limb sometimes because that's where the fruit is. – Will Rogers**

Here we are at the start of a new week with new fruit to pick.

How often do we go out on a limb, either for ourselves or for others? It's easy to go out on that limb when you see the fresh, beautiful-looking fruit at the end of that limb. It's a little harder to go out there when the fruit is obscured, and you don't know what is at the end of that limb. You don't even know if the limb will support your weight.

Right now, many people are venturing out on that limb in an attempt to build a more just and inclusive society. We may not all be able to go out on that limb, but we can do things to support those who are. We can bring a ladder, a rope, or a tool to help prune away some of the brush that obscures the fruit. We can all do something.

Metaphorically, we can all make a human chain to support each other. That connection, that human chain, can break the bonds of isolation that this pandemic has brought upon us, and that same human chain is what can help make for a more just and inclusive society. Let's face it … if we are all linked on that limb, reaching for the fruit at the end, and one person lets go, we could all fall off that limb.

What limbs will you move out on this week? What fruit will you help another reach?

Inching along with you on the limb.

Eugene

Good Morning

How do you take your coffee?

**When traveling with someone, take large doses of patience and tolerance with your morning coffee. – Helen Hayes**

Let's face it, we are all traveling with somebody whether we are at home sheltering in place or traveling halfway around the world. This life, this world, is all we have in the final analysis, and we have to find ways of traveling better together. I take issue with the idea of tolerance. I am against tolerance. The people who schooled me in the world of diversity told me that with tolerance, there are those who are tolerated and those that do the tolerating. In my mind, there is an inequity there. Who gets to decide who is tolerated and who is not? Maybe the better word is inclusion. We need large doses of inclusion with our morning coffee as we travel through this life.

I also never underestimate the value of patience. Just like any skill, the effort towards diversity, inclusion, and building a just and equitable society will take time. People will need to take the time to reevaluate their values and attitudes. People (read: me) need to be schooled in so many things to help bring this about.

Both the ones doing the schooling and those being schooled need to be patient with each other and themselves. Change is hard, and the changes that are needed are no less so.

With patience, goodwill, and a realization we all want the best for our society, we can *all* enjoy the coffee.

Who will you be drinking your coffee? Who will be passing you those large doses of patience and inclusion to add to that brew?

Sitting with you and drinking the coffee of justice.

Eugene

Good Morning

Who or what is being held down?

- **Everybody knows there is no fineness or accuracy of suppression; if you hold down one thing, you hold down the adjoining. – Saul Bellow**

I was thinking about how true Mr. Bellow's statement is. If we try to suppress any person, group of people, or an idea, we end up suppressing a whole lot more … maybe even ourselves.

But let's turn this around. What happens when we try to elevate and support each other? Won't the same hold true? If we reach out in compassion, inclusion, and as an ally, that must have some sort of knock-on effect. Maybe our work will encourage others to do the same. Perhaps the people or groups being supported will be able to bring others along.

Through the smallest of acts of compassion, inclusion, and support during a time of pandemic and social change, we can propagate much more than we thought could be accomplished. What can be achieved is bounded only by one's creativity. The more we support each other, the more we bind ourselves to others' destinies, the further that boundary gets pushed.

No doubt this takes courage. It is the courage of the small hours shown in the smallest of ways. It is the courage that acknowledges that one stands on the shoulders of other courageous people from ages past to our own time in creating a fit society where all can flourish.

The net-net of all this is that raising others, not in a condescending way, is not a zero-sum game. Who will you be raising up today?

Joined with you in raising and supporting each other.

Eugene

Good Morning

How is your portfolio? Where are you making your investments?

- **Invest in the human soul. Who knows, it might be a diamond in the rough. – Mary McLeod Bethune**

People like to talk about investing, whether it is their money or their time, or their talent. Where we make our investments is a reflection of who we are.

The investments that Ms. Bethune is talking about are not the investments shown on a balance sheet or in an account statement. These investments are those that we make in the souls of each other. We can make those investments in many ways, but the key to those investments is that they come from deep within. Every time we reach out to somebody in compassion, understanding, and inclusion, we are investing somebody else's soul.

Conversely, when somebody shares with us an experience, sometimes a painful experience, they are investing in our soul. The ability to be compassionate and listen attentively to somebody else's story is vital if we are going to build a just and inclusive society.

These days of pandemic and social change are challenging, but it is now, more than ever, that we need to make those investments in other people just as others will make investments in us.

If we fail to make those investments, we will end up with a pretty poor balance sheet in the final analysis.

Whose soul will you be investing in today? Who will you let invest in your soul

With you in building up society's portfolio.

Eugene

Good Morning

Let's wind up this work week on an optimistic note.

- **Optimism is the faith that leads to achievement. Nothing can be done without hope and confidence. – Helen Keller**

No significant movement, individual achievement, or social progress occurs without the hope and confidence of those who are bold enough to try and make it happen.

We as a society are beset with many challenges to help bring about a just and inclusive society. For this to come about, we need to rely not only on people's skills and talent but also on their hope and confidence. Maybe hope and confidence are the more important virtues.

As I try and build a better society, I need to look into somebody else's eyes and see their hope and confidence. That hope and confidence might help me "over the hump," as I might say. This hope and confidence can become pervasive as more and more people manifest their hope and confidence in their actions.

Maybe the bottom line is that we all need to believe in each other, in each other's goodwill and good intentions. Some (read: me) may not be the most skilled, but as long as I can tap into others' hope and confidence and let others draw from my hope and confidence, we won't be far off the mark.

Hope and confidence, even in the face of setbacks and opposition, will become the pearl of great price as we move forward together to create a more just and inclusive society. Sharing hope and confidence with you.

Eugene

Good Morning

What great ideal are you striving towards?

- **It is a useless life that is not consecrated to a great ideal. It is like a stone wasted on the field without becoming a part of any edifice. – Jose Rizal**

Interestingly, Mr. Rizal uses the term "consecrate". Part of the definition of that word means "to set apart," typically for service to a deity. I think, in this context, it means more than just being dedicated to a cause. In some way, the cause or ideal becomes transcendent.

The times we are living now need such consecration. If we are to build a just and inclusive society, if we are to break the bonds of isolation caused by this pandemic, we must find the means within ourselves to make that consecration. Times and circumstances in the past have called for such consecration. That time is upon us again.

Some of us can be huge stones in the edifice that we build; some can be smaller stones, but large or small, all are needed to build a firm and lasting edifice. We all have skills and talents, and they all can be used.

What sort of edifice will you help build today?

United with you in consecration.

Eugene

# 24 June 2020

Good Morning

I'm sorry I missed getting a note out yesterday. I was having serious technical issues, but … today is another day.

- **With the new day comes new strength and new thoughts. – Eleanor Roosevelt**

Every day we are given a new opportunity. We have the choice of using it to brood over yesterday or fantasize about tomorrow. There seems to be an urgency in what Mrs. Roosevelt is saying. An urgency to use today's strength and thoughts to make a better world, a more just and inclusive society.

During this time of social change and pandemic, the work that we are given is to break down isolation, change structures and attitudes by reaching out in a spirit of compassion and inclusion to foster positive change in our world. That work takes strength and creativity of thought. The strength that is called for may not be physical strength but a strength of character and will to do the sometimes difficult and uncomfortable work that must be done to create new tomorrows for others that will shine with justice and inclusivity.

The inner strength is needed because there will be difficulties, setbacks, and failures. We must not let those set us back and sap our strength.

How will you be using your new strength today? What new thoughts will you make manifest?

Joined with you in strength.

Eugene

Good Morning

It's good to be up and about and see new things … but how new are they, *really*?

- **The real voyage of discovery consists not in seeking new landscapes, but in having new eyes. – Marcel Proust**

The current pandemic and its social changes have caused us all to see things; things we may not have thought existed anymore, things within ourselves that we felt we had neatly dealt with and tucked away. Maybe those things in society and ourselves were always there, but we did not have the eyes to see.

The question now is, what do we do with what we are seeing? The genie is out of the bottle. There is no going back to a comfortable life behind a nice big hedge that blocks out anything we don't want to deal with. I'm reminded of the early days of the battle of Normandy in World War II. The Allied tanks and troops were having difficulty advancing because of the thick hedgerows that dotted the landscape and provided excellent cover for the enemy. It was only after somebody developed a prong that could be welded to the front of the tanks that they were able to break through the hedgerows.

Every time we reach out in solidarity and compassion to somebody else, we break through the hedge. Every time we take action to help create a more just and inclusive society, we break through the hedge. Our individual actions may not break through in total, but everyone will make a breakthrough with their individual actions.

What hedge will you break through today?

Joined with you in seeing with new eyes.

Eugene

Good Morning

What will you be plowing today?

- **In times of great stress or adversity, it's always best to keep busy, to plow your anger and your energy into something positive. – Lee Iacocca**

We are at the start of a new week and a shortened week for many of us due to the Independence Day holiday, so there might be an urgency to get things done. There is a difference between being busy with work and having busywork.

It is vital that we need to focus on spending our energies on something positive, now more than ever. We can get wrapped up in the pain that many in the world or even our own households are experiencing. Their pain is not trivial. How we respond to their pain as well as our own is going to have huge impacts.

What positive thing will you be putting your energies into today?

Teamed with you at the plow.

Eugene

Good Morning

What class are you in?  What class have people said you are in?

- **You have to be taught to be second class; you're not born that way. – Lena Horn**

-

We all have different stations in life, based on education, and opportunities presented, and birth.  Some people work with their hands, other work with their minds.  One is not better than the other.  Both are necessary for the functioning of society.

Your station in life has nothing to do with the class you were born.  We were all born into the *first* (and only) class.  We all have inherent dignity and value.  This time of pandemic and social change has highlighted the different stations that we occupy and has brought those differences into sharp and sometimes uncomfortable focus. Still, in the final analysis, we are all members of one class: the *human class*.

We have got to find ways to break the isolation that one's station or circumstances in life can bring about.  We must reach out to each other in equality, compassion, and inclusion to build a society where everyone's inherent human dignity and class can be brought into full flower.

Whose dignity and class will you be affirming today?

Sitting next you in the first class lounge.

Eugene

# JULY 2020

Good Morning

The famous comic, actor, director, and screenwriter Carl Reiner passed away this week

- **The key to longevity is to interact with other people. – Carl Reiner**

This time of pandemic and social change has brought into sharp focus the need for all of us to interact with others. Some people choose solitude and some have it forced upon them.

In the history of the early Christian church, there was a tradition of hermits who would live a secluded life, but it is interesting to note that most of the stories of these great mystics start with, "so and so went up the mountain to see the hermit," so even in their seclusion, these individuals received and met others. In more modern times, the Benedictine monks have a tradition of hospitality. It is written into their rule of life. These same Benedictine monks are also known for brewing beer and making liqueur (Bénédictine). You cannot convince me that all these wonderful beverages were meant just for the monks in the monastery.

Now that social distancing restrictions are starting to ease, maybe we need to think about a more radical hospitality. A hospitality that may take us further afield; one that goes beyond just being nice to the neighbor on the other side of the fence, one that takes risks to reach out to others in compassion and inclusion to create a better society. This radical hospitality is not just "let's all play nice in the sandbox". It is a hospitality that fundamentally shapes and redefines how we include others. This type of hospitality calls for risk, but in my opinion, it is a risk worth taking lest we fall back into a comfortable tribalism. If we do so, nothing will change.

How will you be radically hospitable today?

Sitting with you and sipping Bénédictine.

Eugene

Good Morning

Let's take a walk in the orchard.

- **A tree is known by its fruit; a man by his deeds. A good deed is never lost; he who sows courtesy reaps friendship, and he who plants kindness gathers love. – Saint Basil**

We're coming into the summer. Soon the fruit trees will be coming out with all manner of fruit. So it is with life. Each one of us has the opportunity to produce good fruit or fruit of inferior quality. The question now becomes how do we reap good fruit. Every time we reach out in solidarity, compassion, and inclusion, we create a fertile environment for good fruit. But let's take the analogy a little further. Good fruit in an orchard does not come in isolation. Since trees in an orchard are planted in basically the same soil, if the soil is developed, all the trees will benefit.

So it is with society. The more each one of us makes an effort to plant kindness, even the smallest action, there will be rich bounty at the harvest. This time of pandemic and social unrest may have caused some of us to withdraw, turn inwards, but now, more than ever, we must think about developing the orchard; to sow kindness, justice, and inclusion. The upcoming holiday may be a great time to do that sowing.

What seeds will you be sowing? What fruit trees will you be cultivating?

Walking with you in the orchards.

Eugene

Good Afternoon

Do you feel overwhelmed, or are you doing the overwhelming?

- **Do your little bit of good where you are; it's those little bits of good put together that overwhelm the world. – Desmond Tutu**

I think it is interesting the Archbishop Tutu uses the word overwhelm instead of vanquish, or beat, or some other term that implies the imposition of one's will on another. To me, the use of the word overwhelm implies a moral force; a force that does not beat an opponent but wins them over. It could be argued that perhaps what Archbishop Tutu is referring to is what Mahatma Gandhi referred to as satyagraha or "truth force".

It's also interesting that Archbishop Tutu talks about little bits of good; not massive undertakings of good, but the good we can do simply, in the everyday, in the regular course of our lives. When added together with everyone else's small acts of compassion, each small act of compassion, inclusion, and solidarity will indeed overwhelm the world. The old ways of doing things, old prejudices, the remnants of oppression will be overwhelmed, and a new society will come out. It may not happen today or tomorrow, and it won't happen without setbacks, but I am certain that it won't happen at all unless we, individually, start taking seriously the need for each of us to contribute to the creation of that new society by the accumulation of small acts of compassion, solidarity and inclusion that our society is so desperately in need of. What bits of good will you be putting together today?

Partnering with you in little bits of good.

Eugene

Good Afternoon

It's a holiday weekend, so you get a bonus: two quotes to think about.

- **The greatness of America lies not in being more enlightened than any other nation, but rather in her ability to repair her faults. – Alexis de Tocqueville**

- **The highest patriotism is not a blind acceptance of official policy, but a love of one's country deep enough to call her to a higher plain. – George McGovern**

On a holiday like this, it's easy just to sit back and think about the past. We think about the Founding Fathers (and Mothers), and we look at them through the rose-colored glasses of schoolbook history lessons or their great oratory. The reality is that these people were complicated humans, just as we all are, with aspects of their personal lives that we, in this day and age, find troubling.

I think the meaning of this holiday has to be forward-thinking. What Mr. McGovern and Monsieur de Tocqueville both seem to be talking about is that true patriotism lies in moving the country forward to a more just and inclusive society. It's easy to be a patriot when you have been able to reap the benefits of this great land, but what about those who have not? How can we express our love of our country in full voice when the voices and experiences of many have been ignored or marginalized?

I know I have said this before, but this pandemic and the social change being wrought is going to be the rise and fall of many in this nation. I think those that will rise will be the ones who hear the clarion call to reach out to others in compassion, hope, and inclusion to build a better, more just society.

Enjoy the holiday but don't let it be an end to something. Let it be the springboard to the building of a better nation.

Joining with you in moving to the higher plain.

Eugene

Good Morning

I hope everyone had a good holiday rest. Now, it's back to "the grind" with its myriad of concerns and fears. How will you respond to them?

- **I've been absolutely terrified every moment of my life - and I've never let it keep me from doing a single thing I wanted to do. – Georgia O'Keefe**

Ms. O'Keefe exemplifies something I have said before. She did not take counsel of her fears. She didn't ignore them; she acknowledged they existed and still moved forward. Maybe that's the key. Some people will dismiss their fears as if they don't exist, but if we are honest with ourselves about our fears, maybe that is the first step to moving forward.

Being honest about our fears is also necessary if we are going to be honest with others. This pandemic has been a cause of great anxiety for everyone. Now, more than ever, we need to be honest with each other if we are going to have any chance of building a more inclusive and compassionate society. Being able to express fears and uncertainty entails much personal risk. Maybe we can take a page from Ms. O'Keefe's experience. If she was not honest with herself about her fears, she might not have produced the great works she did.

The key to all this is being able to see the potential in being open about our hopes … and fears.

How will you keep moving, despite your fears today?

Joined with you in moving forward.

Eugene

Good Morning

It's looking like an average Tuesday in the summer … but is it common?

- **Ain't no man can avoid being born average, but there ain't no man got to be common. – Satchel Paige**

Interestingly, Mr. Paige makes the distinction between being average and being common. To be average generally means that 50% of a given population are higher than you, in terms of some measure, and 50% are lower than you, compared to the same standard. This is simply math but being common is something different.

In this context, I think that being common means to be ordinary, run-of-the-mill, not very special—and that is a whole other kettle of fish. Each one of us is a unique creation with unique gifts and talents. Those should not be taken lightly. We all can influence, in some fashion, the world around us. We have a choice to make. We can influence the world for good or for ill. This time of pandemic and social change will call for the best of us all to bring our gifts and talents to help create a more just, compassionate, and inclusive society.

I would venture that sometimes it's a challenge to find where our talents fit. That path of discovery in and of itself is of value as well. It will entail a broadening of one's perspective and perception, and might lead to the discovery of new talents and gifts. This path to discovery may be rocky and uneven at times, but the trip is well worth it.

Where are you on the road to discovery? What new talents and gifts will you discover? Joined with you in an uncommon life.

Eugene

Good Morning

Is your glass half empty or half full this morning?

- **If one morning I walked on top of the water across the Potomac River, the headline that afternoon would read: 'President Can't Swim.' – Lyndon B. Johnson**

This could be interpreted as a statement on President Johnson's relationship with the press, but maybe he is saying something a little deeper. Often, how we deal with life can be attributed to perspective. Are we operating from a perspective of plenty or a perspective of want? How we deal with the day's challenges, and with each other, can be greatly influenced by that perspective.

When I speak of plenty or want, I am not talking about material plenty or material want. I am thinking about plenty or want in terms of generosity of spirit. I have met people who lived and worked in material want but had incredible generosity of spirit because of their perspective on their daily lives.

That generosity of spirit is what is needed now, more than ever. If we are going to have any hope of coming through this pandemic and the systemic social change we find ourselves in, we have got to be generous in spirt; not only with those we have become comfortable with but also with others we may not otherwise come in contact with. It is in this way, we can build a more just, inclusive, and compassionate society.

What will be your perspective today?

United with you in generosity of spirit.

Eugene

# 9 July 2020

Good Morning

Whose life is yours?

- **You must live for another if you wish to live for yourself. – Lucius Annaeus Seneca**

I recall a beer commercial from many years ago that called for people (men predominantly) to "Go For The Gusto". The image of the strong, self-reliant man is a popular trope in advertising, but is it a helpful one in today's society?

The question now is, what does living for another mean? I'm guessing that the answer is different for each individual. Maybe part of living for others is part of a journey of discovery of who "the other" is. For some, "the other" could be the person down the street, for others, "the other" is a person on the other side of the world. The key is to take the journey seriously, and maybe the best start is to look at "the other" not so much as "the other" but maybe "the equal." Equal in terms of dignity; equal in terms of their value as a human being.

I would submit that living for another is not a one-way street. The fact that you open yourself up to live for another means that somebody, somewhere, somehow is going to be living for you. You can call it reciprocity, or maybe you can simply call it a community—a community of compassion, inclusion, and equity. The times we live in will call upon more community, more openness, and more living for others. For whom will you be living today? How will you be building community?

With you in living for others.

Eugene

Good Morning

We have come to Friday, the end of another work week … or is it?

- **Success is a journey, not a destination. The doing is often more important than the outcome. – Arthur Ashe**

Journeys are funny things. No matter how well we plan and map a route, we end up someplace else. The same can be said about life. In January, when we were looking at the year ahead, most of us thought that every day we would wake up, go to the office, put in a good day's work while the kids were at school, come home at the end of the day and maybe plan some outings for the weekend. But here we, almost four months of sheltering in place and working from home and trying to figure out the social changes going on around us.

But what of the journey that brought us to this place? What have we learned? What have we experienced? Whom have we impacted? Who has impacted us? The answer to all those questions lies not in an outcome but in the journey itself; the process that has led us to this point. What will we do with what we have learned and experienced? How will our interactions with others change us and change them? I would submit that if we don't use all that we have experienced to help create a more just, inclusive, and compassionate society, the journey itself may lack some meaning.

I am reminded of something a general once said. During the Second World War, General Bill Slim and the 14th Army marched and fought through monsoon and malaria in Burma's jungles and arrived at the city of Mandalay in March 1945. The outcome of the war in that part of the world was by no means certain. General Slim said to his troops at that time something to the effect of, "Kipling wrote a very fine poem about the road to Mandalay. I'm not so much interested in the road to Mandalay but the road from Mandalay. Let's get on them and see where they go."

Where is today's journey going to lead? Whom are you going to accompany?

Accompanying you on the road.

Eugene

Good Morning

It a beautiful morning here in Chicago. The weather is excellent for a walk.

- **You have to pick the places you don't walk away from. – Joan Didion**

I've heard the following phrase when a potential interpersonal conflict crops up: "Is this the hill you want to die on?" I guess this phrase's meaning lies in determining if the issue in dispute is worth the effort. We all make those sorts of decisions every day in terms of our personal and professional relationships. This time of physical separation due to the COVID-19 pandemic has made it, in my mind, a lot easier to walk away from things.

But the question is, should we be walking away? Walking away from a person or a situation implies abandonment. It becomes a statement of what we care about and what we don't care about. Let's face it, this time of social unrest and global pandemic can sometimes bring out, if not the worst, maybe the unattractive attributes of our (read: my) character.

Maybe now is the time to be walking towards things and people. If we are to have any hope of creating a more just, compassionate, and inclusive society, we need to move towards each other and situations that might not make us feel the most comfortable. It's only through our willingness to confront and work through our discomfort that we have any chance at personal or societal growth. What will you be waking towards today?

Joined with you in the walk.

Eugene

Good Morning

I'm working out of an upstairs room in my house today, and I miss looking out the big picture window on the first floor, but I know that the beauty is still there.

- **Think of all the beauty still left around you and be happy. – Anne Frank**

It's a testament to this young girl that she still thought about beauty, given the desperate situation she had to endure. It's interesting to note that she speaks about the beauty still left. It's an acknowledgment that there was great ugliness and horror around her, but that there was still beauty even in that.

The use of the word still implies a certain transient nature of that beauty; it could disappear sometime in the future, but it's still around for now.

Each of us has the opportunity to appreciate the beauty that still surrounds us, even in this time of pandemic and social change. There is the visual beauty we can see but also the inner beauty that people exhibit as they move forward, sometimes in a halting way, to the creation of a more just, compassionate, and inclusive society. Sometimes this beauty has to go up against some very ugly forces, but that beauty is still present, still making an impact.

That inner beauty does not exist in a vacuum. It must be nurtured. It's still with us now, but if it is not nurtured, it could disappear. We could then, as Winston Churchill said, "sink into the abyss of a new Dark Age made more sinister, and perhaps more protracted, by the lights of perverted science."

How will you nurture beauty today?

Still with you in fostering beauty.

Eugene

Good Morning

I have been privileged to work among many top-flight attorneys, so the idea of justice has become very important.

- **Justice is conscience, not a personal conscience but the conscience of the whole of humanity. Those who clearly recognize the voice of their own conscience usually recognize also the voice of justice. – Aleksander Solzhenitsyn**

It is interesting how Mr. Solzhenitsyn takes the conscience, which resides in the individual, and draws out the larger societal imperative of justice. Maybe it can be inferred that the lack of justice in many aspects of our world is because we have lost a sense of conscience. Perhaps we have become so outwardly focused on defending a position, a neighborhood, some material object, or some perceived right or privilege, that we have drowned out that voice of conscience which makes us truly human and binds us together, each to the other.

Mr. Solzhenitsyn is also saying that justice is not some "out there" abstraction. The fundamentals of justice are within each of us. The question now is, are we going to listen to that voice of conscience, even if it will make things a little less comfortable for us?

In life, bargains must always be struck. How are we going to strike the bargain with our conscience? If we are going to have any hope of creating a more just, compassionate, and inclusive world, we have to start thinking about listening to the voice of conscience and letting that voice be formed by other noble and honest voices. To do this, we must all walk a moral tightrope.

How do we find the authentic voices to form our conscience and avoid the carnival barkers whose only goal is to swindle and cheat?

Joined with you in recognizing the voice of justice.

Eugene

# 16 July 2020

Good Morning

What kind of community are we building?

- **This world of ours... must avoid becoming a community of dreadful fear and hate, and be, instead, a proud confederation of mutual trust and respect – Dwight D. Eisenhower**

There is an old saying in Chicago: "We don't want nobody nobody sent". The meaning here is, that if somebody was looking for a job on the city payroll, you needed a sponsor, somebody connected who would vouch for you (and your willingness to do political work in exchange for the job). The inference is that if you were an outsider, you did not have a chance.

But now, can we afford to leave anyone on "the outside"? The question now before us is whether or not we will look beyond our block or neighborhood or city and reach out and build that confederation that President Eisenhower talks about. Right now, we have two great forces at play. We have the global COVID-19 pandemic, which has required us to retreat and shelter in place physically. We also have the massive social change that is taking place. Some may want to simply retreat even further, maybe not out of malice, but out of fear. Others will extend themselves and build a community of trust, respect, compassion, inclusion, and justice. I am convinced that even the smallest movement a person takes towards building that confederation will engender more movement by others, and all those small movements by many people, when taken in total, will become something wonderful to behold.

How will you build trust and community today? Walking with you in rejecting fear and hate.

Eugene

Good Morning

The new car that my wife and I own has a feature that lets you know if you are drifting into another lane … which is a good thing, but is such a warning a good thing in life?

- **Who wants to live in a world where you can only stay in the lane of your birth? – Bari Weiss**

Often, when posed with a personal challenge, it is the easy, or at least convenient thing, to do to fall back on what is tried and true. We know what has worked in the past, and that should be sufficient.

But is it sufficient? Any sort of personal growth entails risk. We take risks every day, both large and small. Sometimes the risks pan out, sometimes they don't, but even when they don't pan out, the personal growth and learning can be of immense value.

The times we live in require significant change on many fronts; changes in the way business is conducted, and maybe more importantly, changes in the way we relate to each other as human beings. These changes are not without risk. We risk moving out of a personal comfort zone in the hope of creating a more just, compassionate, and inclusive society. We have to ask ourselves the hard questions about what risks we are willing to take and which we are not.

There is a comfort in all this risk-taking, in that we don't have to go it alone. A wise friend of mine said that we might not be all in the same boat, but we are all in the same storm. It's up to each and every one of us to throw a rope from our boat to somebody else's boat. We may miss the other boat with our rope, and if we reach it, the other person may just toss it back into the sea. We need to keep tossing that rope. Chances are, somebody will catch it, the boats will come closer together, and we'll be better off weathering the storm.

To whom will you be tossing your rope today?  Whose rope will you be catching and pulling?

Joined with you in changing lanes.

Eugene

Good Morning

Here we are on another Monday, with new challenges and old burdens to take up. But maybe it's time to let go of some burdens as well

- **We are one people with one family. We all live in the same house ... and through books, through information, we must find a way to say to people that we must lay down the burden of hate. For hate is too heavy a burden to bear. – John Lewis**

Undoubtedly, the current pandemic has been a significant burden to many people, and the social change has been difficult to watch. I'm thinking that the now, with all manner of change going on, is the most opportune time to lay down our burdens of bias. Let's face it; we are all making many changes in our lives at this moment, so what's one more added to the list? It would be easy to use this time of isolation to retreat even further into tribalism and an attitude of "I've got mine ... I don't have to worry".

Mr. Lewis is absolutely right. We all live in the same house, even if we are isolated because of the pandemic. We need not shoulder the burden of letting go of old burdens alone. Every time we reach out in compassion, justice, and inclusivity, we are making the task of releasing a burden easier. Every time we speak out in truth of how we have grown, how we have become a better person, we are making it easier for somebody to lay down their burden. Every time we move into a space that is not necessarily comfortable for us, we are helping somebody else lose their burden.

What burdens are can you lay down today? What burdens can you help others lay down today?

Laboring with you in the same house to help lay down each other's burden.

Eugene

R.I.P. John Lewis

# 21 July 2020

Good Morning

We are now entering high summer. Many things in the garden are changing, and I am looking forward to heading to southwest Michigan for farm-fresh produce. Even outside of the garden, things are changing in many ways.

- **We can remake the world daily. --Paul Wellstone**

I had the chance to talk with an esteemed friend and colleague yesterday, and this person was talking about her attempts to create community and make an expression of care among her colleagues. I was struck by the fact that she referred to these efforts as, "opening the gates to the playground." That image stuck with me all day. It conjures up images of young people doing what they do best, at a time where the opportunities are limitless. All it took for that to occur was for somebody to open the gate to the playground.

Sometimes the playground gets crowded, and sometimes only a few (or even no one) enters the playground. The key to remember is that you remade the world because you opened the playground. Every time you reach out to an individual in compassion, justice, and inclusion, you have changed the world. Results (good results, that is) would be nice, but the key is the sustained effort to reach out.

I may have shared this with you in the past, but it bears repeating. I am a big believer in the law of averages. I may make 100 attempts to reach out. Ninety-nine of them may have little to show for the effort, but the 100th attempt might reap a huge harvest. Now is the time to make those attempts to break down isolation, foster understanding, and promote justice and inclusion.

What gates will you be opening today?

Walking with you into the playground.

Eugene

Good Morning

It's mid-week, and we all probably have a bunch of people that we have to talk to this week.

- **As soon as I reach any town, I talk to the shoe-shine boys or the barbers or the people in the restaurants, because it's Mr. Joe Doakes who is very close to reality. – Thurgood Marshall**

Justice Marshall makes an excellent point. We (read: me) can frequently be impressed by the words of the high and mighty, but maybe we should be listening to those who maybe are not so high and not so mighty. I think Justice Marshall is implying that the stories of the common person, which frequently are the stories of struggle and overcoming, are what we need to hear to help us break through our zone of comfort. The bottom line is there is much we can learn from each other.

The question now becomes, how do we take up Justice Marshall's challenge to really listen to each other? What concrete actions must we take so that the voices of those long ignored or suppressed find utterance? It must be understood that the voice of the disenfranchised is not something given to them by those in power. It is their birthright.

To build a more just, compassionate, and inclusive society, we must find those voices. We must genuinely hear, without judgment, those voices. We must create opportunities for ourselves to listen to those voices. Sometimes those voices have things to say that may not be the most comfortable but hear them we must. To do otherwise will only create a society with a veneer of justice, compassion, and inclusion.

Who will you be talking to today? Whose voice will you be promoting?

Partnering with you in getting close to reality.

Eugene

Good Morning

We live in an instant society: instant coffee, instant dinners, instant relationships. But is speed all that it's cracked up to be?

- **It does not matter how slowly you go as long as you do not stop. – Confucius**

We all seem to be in a hurry, or at least anxious, for some sort of normalcy to be restored to our lives. I can understand that. We all want to be able to return to the tried and true in certain respects. People are clamoring for social change right now, and they are entitled to that change.

Maybe the thing to keep in mind is that it's not necessarily the speed at which we can bring about change but simply that we move in the direction of a new and brighter future. A future of justice, compassion, and inclusion where everyone's voice is heard and appreciated is where we are trending.

Throughout the arc of human existence, change has only been accomplished by the diligent application to the tasks that have caused new societies to rise and relationships between peoples and communities to grow.

We all have a part to play in bending that arc. Every time we reach out in compassion, every time we try and break down the isolation we and others are going through, we are bending that arc. Sometimes the arc won't bend right now, but the continued effort will bring about its inevitable bending.

The circumstances we are in right now provide us with an excellent opportunity to bring about change. Seize those opportunities that present themselves to you. If you do, you will be able to look back with some satisfaction and know that you helped bring about change, helped break somebody's isolation, and most importantly, affirmed the dignity of somebody else and, by that, affirmed your own dignity.

How will you bend the arc today?

Joining you in not stopping and moving forward.

Eugene

# 24 July 2020

Good Morning

Welcome to the end of the week. I wonder what everyone is thinking about for this weekend … and beyond?

- **A small group of thoughtful people could change the world. Indeed, it's the only thing that ever has. – Margaret Meade**

Interestingly, Ms. Meade talks about a small, thoughtful group of people changing the world. The implication is that change requires thought; it involves group and individual reflection. It's one thing to storm the barricades and demand change now, and it's another thing to really consider what change will be most efficacious.

Change is never easy, but there is solace because we need not go it alone. Many people of good will are looking to create a world of justice, compassion, and inclusion and are trying in ways large and small to break down the isolation that is our part and parcel in these days of the pandemic. The task before us is to find those people of goodwill. We have the tools at hand to do the outreach. All it takes now is the courage to act.

How will you show courage today?

Laboring with you in bringing about thoughtful change.

Eugene

Good afternoon

It's Monday, the start of a new work week, and we once again get to listen to the cacophony that is around us. Maybe that is all background noise to the real battle—the battle within

- **Some of the greatest battles will be fought within the silent chambers of your own soul. – Ezra Taft Benson**

What do we find in the silence of the soul? Ideals, a world of experience, joy and grief, wisdom from others, and a myriad of other things can be found there. Mr. Benson speaks about the silence of the soul but not the solitude of the soul. Many of the great decisions we take are indeed taken alone, but I would submit to you that entering into the silence and solitude of choice is but the last step in what can be a long process of making a decision. The weightier the decision, the longer the "run up" to that decision.

We need not enter into that silent chamber with it being empty, with no tools to help us. I am reminded of a passage from the Gospel of Matthew that reads as follows: "Then every scribe who has been instructed in the kingdom of heaven is like the head of a household who brings from his storeroom both the new and the old." (Matthew 13:52).

So the question now is, how are we building up that storeroom of the soul? Every time we reach out to somebody to break isolation, we are building up our storeroom. Every time we reach out in compassion, justice, and inclusion, we are building up the storeroom. Every time we speak truth to power, we are building up the storeroom.

When we go into that silent chamber, that silent storeroom, we can go in with the confidence that we have built it with wisdom and experience that will allow us to come out of that chamber with a decision or a transformation that does honor our life's experience and will help transform the world.

What will you be adding to your storeroom today?

Rejoicing with you as we share both the old and new from our storeroom.

Eugene

# 28 July 2020

Good Morning

We are all trying to make some sort of difference in the world, which is a good thing, but maybe we also need to think where that difference will be felt.

- **The first question which the priest and the Levite asked was: 'If I stop to help this man, what will happen to me?' But ... the good Samaritan reversed the question: 'If I do not stop to help this man, what will happen to him?'**

Dr. King makes an excellent analysis of the parable of the Good Samaritan. He compares the priest and the Levite, who are inwardly focused, and compares it to the Good Samaritan, who is outwardly focused. It is a question we all must come to grips with. What will happen to "the other" if we don't try to break down isolation, if we don't reach out in justice, compassion and inclusion. We can choose to act or not act. We can choose to ignore the results of inaction, but the results are still there.

Maybe as we consider how to act or not act, we need to consider an additional question. That question is, "If I don't stop to help, what will happen to me?" The question asks us to consider how our lack of action will impact our basic humanity and dignity. How will we be diminished? It is indeed an inwardly-focused question. It asks us to assess our actions or inaction against our own basic humanity. It asks us to consider what we will see in the mirror every morning if we don't act.

I am convinced that every time we reach out to break down isolation, reach out in justice, compassion and inclusion, we are affirming our own basic humanity and dignity and affirming the humanity and dignity of others. The more we can recognize that basic humanity and dignity in others, the more we will be moving towards a better, more noble society. But it has to start somewhere; with you, with me.

How will you change by your acts of compassion today?

Partnering with you in stopping to help.

Eugene

Good Morning

You have all heard the phrase "misery loves company", but is that accurate?

- **What makes loneliness an anguish is not that I have no one to share my burden, but this: I have only my own burden to bear. – Dag Hammarskjold**

I think Mr. Hammarskjold is making a more profound statement that simply "many hands make light the burden." I think he is making a fundamental statement about the human condition, about human capacity. I think his point is that we as humans reach our greatest potential when we engage with each other and the world. We cannot be fully human unless we affirm others' inherent dignity and value, and we do that by reaching out to others.

Let's take Mr. Hammarskjold's words and turn them around. Maybe what makes for joy is that I have my joy and happiness but that I share in the joy and happiness of those around me. Even in the most desperate situations, people find cause to rejoice in the good fortune and new beginnings others are making.

So what's the bottom line here? It seems that the call that Mr. Hammarskjold is making to us all is to reach out in justice, compassion, and inclusion to others. This call would not be unusual for Mr. Hammarskjold because he was the second Secretary General of the United Nations from April 1953 to September 1961.

Every step we take to reach out to others, every phone call we make to check on somebody, every smile we give to the stranger in the street is a hammer strike against the brick wall of isolation, injustice, and exclusion. In those simple actions, we are giving Mr. Hammarskjold's words life.

Whose burdens will you help bear today?

Partnering with you to eliminate loneliness and anguish.

Eugene

Good Morning

My first trip to London in 1978 was when I encountered in the subway the famous phrase, "Mind the gap." It is very ubiquitous in the London tube. You hear it over the loudspeakers, and you see it stenciled on the platform floor. It's a simple phrase and easy to do. I wonder, though, how well we are minding the gap in our world?

- **We have a positive vision of the future founded on the belief that the gap between the promise and reality of America can one day be finally closed. We believe that. – Barbara Jordan**

It's been forty-four years since Ms. Jordan spoke these words at the Democratic National Convention. No doubt we have made progress, but the current circumstances put society at risk of moving backwards. The isolation that many of us have to deal with currently makes it easier to retreat to the tried and true apathy and tribalism.

Even with all that confronts us, there are people, in small and large ways, willing to stand in the gap, willing to bridge that gap, willing to bring about a new society of justice, inclusion, and compassion. We all have choices to make and opportunities to stand in the gap. The more we are willing to stand in the gap, the more the gap will be reduced. Maybe the gap will never be closed. Perhaps as more people stand in the gap, the gap will inch open a little wider. That is no cause of despair. That just provides more opportunities for others to stand in the gap. Every time we reach out to break down isolation, speak truth to power, and demonstrate compassion and inclusion, we are standing in the gap. Not only that but every time we accept somebody's outreach, every time we accept somebody's act of compassion and inclusion, whenever we listen to truth spoken to us, we are also standing in the gap. There is equality and nobility when we all stand in the gap together.

How will you stand in the gap today?

Working with you towards a new promise and new reality.

Eugene

Good Morning

Yesterday, a great American was laid to rest. It might be useful to once more reflect on his words to round out the week.

- **There's nothing wrong with a little agitation for what's right or what's fair. – John Lewis**

There is a well-known word amongst Americans of Italian descent. The word is agita. It's actually not an Italian word, but an Italian-American slang word. It's meant to mean indigestion, but it is often used to refer to anxiety, stress, or aggravation. I am quite sure that Mr. Lewis gave many people agita.

Interestingly, Mr. Lewis uses the phrase "a little agitation." What I see in Mr. Lewis' words is the fact that he acknowledges that everyone can effect change; upset the apple cart, give the powers that be a little agita. Every act of outreach, every act of solidarity, every effort to create a more just, more compassionate, and more inclusive society will undoubtedly give somebody who is very comfortable with the status quo a little agita. As the saying goes, if you are going to dish it out, you need to be able to take it. We all have places where we're comfortable, places where we hope nobody upsets the apple cart. We have to be able to accept a little agita if we are going to dish it out.

Maybe that agita we experience is a good thing. Perhaps it is what we need to help spur us on reaching out, breaking down isolation, and being one more voice calling for justice, compassion, and inclusion. Our actions need not be large or draw lots of attention. The fact that we make the smallest move towards justice, compassion, and inclusion speaks volumes.

How will you be dealing with your agita today?

Conspiring with you to cause a little agitation.

Eugene

# AUGUST 2020

Good Morning

Welcome to a new week and maybe a fresh loaf of bread.

- **There are people in the world so hungry, that God cannot appear to them except in the form of bread. – Mahatma Gandhi**

I'm sure that when Mr. Gandhi said this, he was referring to the grinding poverty in his home country of India. Maybe he was also referring to something more profound.

In the Roman Catholic cycle of gospel readings, this past Sunday was the story of the multiplication of the loaves and fishes. I think there is a great truth here that is useful for people of any, or no faith tradition. In the story, Jesus' close followers ask Him to dismiss the crowds so they can get something to eat. Jesus says to his followers, "Give them some food yourselves." (Matthew 13:16).

I think what Jesus and Mr. Gandhi are doing is challenging all of us to be bread for each other. To be present to the needs of each other. The isolation we have all been experiencing, and the social changes that are going on all around us, call upon us to do what we can to break isolation and help construct a new society of justice, compassion, and inclusion. Sometimes our presence is something somebody may need even more than bread.

Like there is a myriad of bread types, so is it with how we can be present to others. It's up to each of us now to discern what skills and gifts we have and how they can be bread for others. How will you be bread for somebody today? Working with you in the bakery.

Eugene

Good Morning

We've all had the experience of having to throw away a moldy loaf of bread. Maybe something can be learned about that loaf of bread.

- **If they can make penicillin out of moldy bread, they can sure make something out of you. – Muhammed Ali**

Mr. Ali (aka The Champ or The G.O.A.T.) makes a very salient point. It goes beyond the "reduce, reuse, recycle" adage. I think he is making a statement about the nature of the human condition. He is challenging us to find value in everyone. This time of pandemic response and social change compels us to make those connections that will enable us to find value in each other. This task is not a trivial one. We all know people for whom it is challenging to find value. Still, I am convinced that only by finding value in others can we genuinely affirm their humanity and dignity, and in that affirmation, we find our own dignity and humanity. This dignity is the foundation stone of a society based on justice, compassion, and inclusion. We have a chance now, while things are difficult, to lay those foundation stones because, human nature being what it is, we may not be willing to do it when times are good, and we are nice and comfortable.

We can also be very hard on ourselves. Mr. Ali is again calling upon us to change our thinking about ourselves. There may be areas in our lives that we think are just like moldy bread, of no use to anyone. The challenge for us is to look honestly at our brokenness, our mental and emotional baggage, and with a combination of introspection and outreach to others, transform that brokenness and baggage into something useful for ourselves and society. It takes a great deal of courage to do that.

How will you make something out of your baggage and brokenness today?

Working with you in the lab to make penicillin.

Eugene

# 5 August 2020

Good Morning

It feels like I have been stuck in the bakery for the last few days ... which is not bad.

- **Most of my time as a legislator, I served in the minority. So I'm used to getting the heel of a loaf of bread. – Kate Brown**

When I was young, our family purchased a large loaf of French bread every day or so. It made great sandwiches. I always remember wanting the heel of the loaf, or as we called it, the knob end. It was something my brother and I would, on occasion, squabble over. To us, the heel was a desirable thing, to others, not so much. I guess it all depends on one's perspective. In Italian, there is a phrase for the heel of the bread. I won't repeat it here because it is rather rude. Even today, when I order a sandwich, I always ask for the heel of the bread.

Now, this may sound like I am suggesting that people settle. I am doing no such thing. People should strive for whatever part of the loaf they feel is best for them. For some, it is the center of the loaf; for some, it is the heel. Under no circumstances should people be relegated to a certain part of the loaf, nor should somebody tell somebody else what part of the loaf they should get because "they know best." The same is true for a person's place in society, their essential humanity, and inherit dignity.

As this is true with a loaf of bread, the same is true with society. In this time of pandemic response and social change, it is incumbent on us to contribute to a society based on justice, compassion, and inclusion. Everyone can flourish and enjoy their part of the loaf. We all have a vital role to play in making and baking the loaf. If somebody does not make their contribution, the loaf, and society, are diminished by it.

What will you do to contribute to today's loaf of bread?

Enjoying with you the smells of the bakery.

Eugene

# 6 August 2020

Good Morning

Let's have one more day with bread … why not?

- **The art of bread making can become a consuming hobby, and no matter how often and how many kinds of bread one has made, there always seems to be something new to learn. – Julia Child**

For better or for worse, this is the 100th message that I have put out. I hope people are still finding value, comfort, and some food for thought from them. I think what Mrs. Child said about bread applies equally to life. This pandemic response and social change have caused many (read: me) to rethink old positions and ways of thinking. I would like to think that, in this time, we have all grown in some way.

The question now becomes, what will we do with these new learnings and ways of thinking? To continue with the bread analogy, every day is a chance to bake a fresh loaf of bread; another opportunity to integrate what we learned in yesterday's baking to improve today's baking. We don't have to have the same loaf every day. Some days we may want a light sandwich loaf, and another day we might want crusty French bread. How are we going break and share the bread we bake with others? How will we take what we have learned, either in baking or in life, to create a society based on justice, compassion, and inclusion where everyone's life, and the loaf of bread they bring, is celebrated?

Maybe it's been good that we have been lingering in the bakery with the bread (metaphorically) the past few days because it harkens to some of the basic life activities; being at table and sharing the good things of the earth and the labor of our hands. In other words, it is being family to each other.

How will you improve the loaf you bake today?

Joined with you in breaking bread.

Eugene

Good Morning

Happy Friday. We've come to the end of another week with the hope of a restful weekend and a better week next week.

- **Hope begins in the dark, the stubborn hope that if you just show up and try to do the right thing, the dawn will come. You wait and watch and work: you don't give up. – Anne Lamott**

Hope, like courage, is often found in the dark, in the small hours of the morning in the silence on one's heart and surrounding. The question is, what happens when the dawn breaks and the cacophony of the day begins?

Ms. Lamott speaks about a stubborn hope, a hope that is often battered and bruised by experience and the voice of the naysayers, whomever they may be. That stubborn, recalcitrant hope that, when it takes hold, compels us to do the right thing. It is the hope that puts iron in a person's soul and even in defeat – and there will be defeats – will leave them with a brave memory. This hope is the sentinel that waits for the dawn, the dawn of a better day, a better society based on justice, compassion, and inclusion.

In this time of pandemic and social change, we all need this stubborn, recalcitrant hope. That stubborn hope will cause people to continue reaching out, to break down isolation, ferment compassion and inclusion, and render new social structures based on justice. It is a hope that compels, challenges, and makes demands. How will you respond to the voice of stubborn hope today? With you in keeping watch and not giving up.

Eugene

# 10 August 2020

Good Morning

Happy Monday. We are at the start of a new week of sheltering in place, and there is fresh news of looting here in Chicago. I know people are wondering when all this will end.

- **Great works are performed not by strength but by perseverance. – Samuel Johnson**

Dr. Johnson makes a good point that we need perseverance if we are to do anything worthwhile. There is an old saying that sometimes we all have to "keep on keeping on," which is a more modern rendering of Dr. Johnson's sentiments.

All that being said, I would submit that one of the knock-on effects of perseverance is internal, moral, and psychological strength. We see all around us the results of isolation, injustice, exclusion, and a lack of compassion. We must persevere and continue to show compassion, break down isolation, and work towards building a society based on justice and inclusion. The more we persist in this, the more strength we will gain to weather the storms ahead (and there will be storms).

We must persevere in the creation of a new society, and new social structures and institutions, because if we don't, we run the risk of returning to the old ways of living; to the old tribalism of the past and an attitude of "nobody gave me anything so I don't owe anybody anything".

There is another old saying about a dog with a bone. Usually, the dog that ends up with the bone is not necessarily the biggest dog but the one that holds the longest. It's that unrelenting, dogged, stubborn perseverance that is called for now. It may not be pretty, but in the long-run, it can get the job done. To put it more bluntly, we have to be that dog that sinks its teeth into that bone and won't let go.

What will you be sinking your teeth into today?

Partnering with you in the creation of a great work.

Eugene

Good Morning

There is an old saying about the unexamined life is not worth living. What about the indifferent life?

- **Our obligation is to give meaning to life and in doing so to overcome the passive, indifferent life. – Elie Wiesel**

As I sit here in my dining room writing these words, it is easy to think that not much extends beyond the dining room window. It's all nice and green and tree-lined; a perfect summer morning. The reality is that, beyond those tree-lined streets, there are other homes, some very close and some not so close, where life is a daily struggle. Even in affluent neighborhoods, the battle of isolation relentlessly continues. In other places, the struggles for justice, compassion, and inclusion rage unabated.

In this time and place, giving meaning to one's life means doing what one can to break down isolation and work towards a society of justice, compassion, and inclusion. By shattering our indifference, we can give meaning to our own lives and the lives of others. As I have said before, this time of social change and pandemic response will be the rise and fall of many. I am convinced that those that will rise will be the ones that have found a way to give meaning to their lives and the lives of others.

How will you give meaning to your life and the life of others today?

Laboring with you in overcoming the passive, indifferent life.

Eugene

# 12 August 2020

Good Morning

How are you feeling today? Maybe the bigger question is, how are you making others feel today?

- **I've learned that people will forget what you said, people will forget what you did, but people will never forget how you made them feel. – Maya Angelou**

We've all heard the phrase, "actions speak louder than words." That is correct, but what I think Ms. Angelou is asking us to do is look deeper at our words and actions. She is asking us to look at the visible results and what our words and actions have made people feel inside. Have we done or said things that help break down isolation, allowing people on the outside, who are not a part of the "in-group" to truly belong? Have our words and actions affirmed inside of somebody else their inherent dignity, value, and self-worth?

If we are not doing that in our personal and professional lives, how will we bring about a new society based on justice, compassion, and inclusion? The opportunities to make people feel better about themselves, to affirm their value and dignity, are limitless. This is not just, "let's all hold hands and play nice in the sandbox." What I think Ms. Angelou is calling us to is deep and abiding compassion for others. This is hard work, especially in a society that often looks upon people as simply a means to an end. Ms. Angelou is reminding us that people are not a means to an end. They are the beginning and end and the entire journey. How will you make somebody else feel today? Continuing on the journey of affirming the value of others.

Eugene

Good Morning

Recently I went to the hospital for a cardiac exam. Everything is fine, but the reality is that one day, my heart will stop.

- **I believe every human has a finite number of heartbeats. I don't intend to waste any of mine. – Neil Armstrong**

I remember some syrupy ballad from long ago about "turning on your heart light." I have no idea what that meant, but I think it might be somewhat related to what Mr. Armstrong said. His comment strikes me as having an urgency to it. Let's face it: a heartbeat lasts but a moment. It is very fleeting, but all those heartbeats strung together make up a person's life. The question is, how and what are we doing with each one of those heartbeats?

Similarly, maybe Mr. Armstrong is saying that we can accomplish a lot in a small amount of time. Every small act of compassion and inclusion makes a big difference. Every time we make a stand, however small, for justice, we are making a difference.

I think there is a warning in Mr. Armstrong's words as well. Nobody has the same number of heartbeats. The opportunity to show compassion and inclusion towards any one particular person may not be there at a later time. I think Mr. Armstrong is asking us to capitalize on those opportunities *now* and not wait.

What will you be doing with your heartbeats today?

Joined with you in not wasting time.

Eugene

# 14 August 2020

Good Morning

Sometimes I think we live in a world of simulators with virtual reality, virtual meetings, virtual worship services, and sadly, virtual deaths.

- **Even though NASA tries to simulate launch, and we practice in simulators, it's not the same - it's not even close to the same. – Sally Ride**

How often in life do we find ourselves just going through the motions or, as some would say, phoning it in? In other words, how often are we simulating life and not really living it? It happens to us all; the daily grind and the stress of contemporary life often make us all feel (read: me) like just doing enough to get by.

The reality is that this life is not a simulation. I remember going to an engraver and asking him to engrave something; we both said that this engraving was a "one-shot deal." The engraving had to be right, or the item would be worthless. It's the same with our life. We only have one chance to live it honestly. I'm not saying we have to *be* right all the time, but we need to put the effort in, always put our best foot forward, not just go through the motions, not simulate a life, to not phone it in.

Every time we reach out in solidarity, compassion, justice, and inclusion, we are getting it right. We will stumble on the way, but as somebody once said, we showed up, we took a stand, we didn't simulate it.

How will you *not* be simulating it today?

Joined with you in hanging up the phone and not phoning it in.

Eugene

# 17 August 2020

Good Morning

We are at the start of another week, and with it comes a chance to create a new path, a new vision.

- **Forget about trying to compete with someone else. Create your own pathway. Create your own new vision. – Herbie Hancock**

We all live in a hypercompetitive world. Often, everything we seem to be involved in is a zero-sum game; for me to win, you have to lose, but does it have to be that way? The way I see it, if we are always in competition with each other, we are always outwardly focused; we are looking at the other person to know if they are "gaining" on us.

What's the cost of continually trying to beat the other guy? What does it cost us internally, in terms of our essential humanity? Maybe a better use of effort would be to survey the landscape and determine for ourselves what is the best path for us. How can we create a vision and a way for ourselves that leads to a compassionate, just, and inclusive world? Shared goals and objectives are not a bad thing, but I think that each person's creativity should allow them to figure a pathway that best suits them. A by-product of creating one's path is that the journey itself becomes more meaningful, and the insights gained along the way are more profound.

We also don't have to go it alone on our pathway. Many times, pathways will cross; provide opportunities for personal growth, maybe a change in direction. Sometimes, the best path to a particular goal is not a straight line.

This time of social change and pandemic response has sharpened our needs for a more compassionate, just, and inclusive world.

We have an opportunity now to figure a pathway for ourselves that will lead to that goal.

How will you create your own pathway today?

Greeting you as our paths cross.

Eugene

Good Morning

It's fun to be with the "in" crowd. It can be helpful to know such people. When I was growing up, one of the most beneficial things you could say when somebody had a problem was, "I got a guy." But what about everyone else?

- **Most of us don't want to be outsiders – Julian Fellows**

We all remember our school days and the "cool kids" who were part of the "in" crowd. Everyone wanted to know them; everyone wanted their approval. Maybe some of us were part of the "in" crowd. Then there were the others: those who were always on the outside looking in, those who never seemed to measure up. These people often ate lunch alone, were the last to be picked for anything, and generally treated as invisible.

I realize I am speaking in broad generalities, but we tend to cluster with people like us. We cluster ourselves in many ways: by race, religion, zip code, or a host of other things.

The problem with grouping is that there is, by definition, some on the inside and some on the outside. Our society is going through changes that force many of us (read: me) to consider where we belong, who have we included, and maybe more importantly, whom we have excluded. The global COVID-19 pandemic and the societal changes that are going on have brought into stark reality who are on the inside and who have been left on the outside.

I am absolutely convinced that we will be judged personally and professionally in part by whom we have chosen to include in our life, in our work, and in how we approach the greater society.

We can only create a society that is just and compassionate by being more inclusive, not tolerant. The dynamic of tolerance, by definition, means there are the ones that do the tolerating and those that are tolerated. It is an unequal dynamic. Inclusion requires both parties to look upon the other as equal, equal in dignity, equal in humanity.

Starting from the foundation of inclusion, we can move forward to create a more just and compassionate society. It won't happen overnight, but it won't happen at all unless we make a start.

Who will you be including today?

Joined with you on the inside.

Eugene

# 19 August 2020

Good Morning

Yesterday, I had the opportunity to go to the cemetery. It was my mom's first birthday since she died this past April, so I went to her crypt and said some prayers. I also made the rounds of other friends and relatives that were buried in that cemetery. I walked away, thankful for all that those people I visited did for me and meant to me. On further reflection, I have the feeling that they are calling me to be courageous and continue forward.

- **Sometimes even to live is an act of courage. – Lucius Annaeus Seneca**

We live in challenging times. That goes without saying. We are dealing with a pandemic response and fundamental societal change. People are being forced to move from the tried and true into a new dynamic where relationships are changing, where new institutions are coming into their own, and older ones are fundamentally changing. It would be easy for any of us to simply hunker down and wait for all this to blow over, to adopt a bunker mentality.

The alternative to the bunker mentality is to see how the gifts and skills each of us can help create a society based on compassion, justice, and inclusion. I can only wonder what all those buried in the cemetery that I visited would make of the world's situation and what they would give to be a part of it.

We must have the courage not only to move forward to a new reality but to understand that if we are going to have any chance of making a new society, one that is fit for all to live and thrive, and one that honors the memory of our ancestors, we *must* move forward together. We'll get nowhere if we think we can go it alone.

What will be your act of courage today?

Joined with you in living today to the fullest.

Eugene

Good Morning

There is something to be said for long-range planning. I remember in graduate school learning about certain companies in Japan with a very old lineage who not only have five- and ten-year plans but have 100- and 150-year plans. There is also value in trying to address challenges in the here and now.

- **There is never time in the future in which we will work out our salvation. The challenge is in the moment; the time is always now. – James Baldwin**

There's no doubt that we are being challenged at this very moment. The pandemic and its response challenge us, we are challenged by the needed societal change that is going on around us, but I am convinced that there is a more dangerous, more insidious challenge that we all face, and face every day. It is the challenge of inaction; of trying to wait things out until they return to normal, the bunker mentality challenge, as I have said before.

I am convinced that today's challenges can only be met by first acknowledging that we need each other. We need each other's wisdom and moral courage if we will have any hope of building a just, compassionate and inclusive society. This is not just the work of governments or of rich and powerful. Any person of goodwill can do this work. The tasks and the journey will be difficult, but the first step on that journey is to seize the moment *now*. We cannot wait for some great solution to descend from the heavens. The true foundation to a just, compassionate and inclusive society is within the heart and mind, and spirit of those who will make it a reality.

What time is it now, for you?

With you in seizing the moment.

Eugene

Good Morning Everyone

It's Friday, and the weekend is nearly upon us. It's time to relax.

- **When you are at home, even if the chicken is a little burnt, what's the big deal? Relax. – Jacques Pepin**

Mr. Pepin makes a very poignant point about what home should be like. Home should be where you can let your hair down, where people accept you the way you are, warts and all. Home is not the place where you have to constantly put on the "bella figura".

Maybe Mr. Pepin has a message for our broader life. Everything we do in life will be a little rough around the edges in some way. Perhaps that's what adds personality to it. I remember many years ago traveling for work and eating in hotels … a lot. It seemed to me that every time something arrived from room service, the presentation was perfect. The hamburger had exactly four evenly placed grill marks, and the patty fit precisely on the bun; the pickle slices were precisely the same, and there were precisely twenty-one French fries on the plate. After a while, the food lacked any sort of character. You started longing for the oddly shaped burger, the slightly overdone pork chop, the chicken that's a little burnt on the edges.

We all come with our burnt edges and odd shapes, in other words, our differences. It is in those differences, in our lack of conformity, in our different perspectives, in our *diversity* that the real strength of the human spirit shines forth. Maybe Mr. Pepin is calling for us to relax, in general, about our imperfections and let the gifts and skills we have be brought forth to help create a more just, compassionate, and *inclusive* society.

There is an old adage that a stopped clock is right at least twice a day, so the chances are that we may be right at least some of the time, even with our imperfections.

We need not be perfect to show up.  We just need to show up *with* our imperfections.

How will you show up today?

Enjoying life with its slightly burnt ends.

Eugene

Good Afternoon

I know this message is a little late today, but things got busy early on. Maybe it's good to reflect what we get busy with.

- **While I am busy with little things, I am not required to do greater things. – Saint Francis de Sales**

Contemporary life is busy and noisy, with so many demands on our time and talents. We all need to take stock and look at who and what are making demands on us. We need to be able to prioritize.

I also think St. Francis is saying something more profound. How often have we gotten involved in something as a way to avoid something? What are we avoiding? What would we rather not do? I think it is interesting that St. Francis uses the comparative greater versus the adjective great. Greatness is all a matter of perspective. One person's greater thing may not be a greater thing for somebody else. Many mystics from numerous religious traditions have spoken about using the everyday and ordinary as a path to holiness. I would submit to you that, at this time, maybe the greater thing is to do that one small action that is going to break down isolation, that will speak truth to power, that will help bring about a more just, compassionate, and inclusive society. No doubt some days it's going to be more challenging than others to do that one small action but do it anyway. It will put us one step closer to a new society.

What will be your greater thing today?

Joined with you in finding the greater thing.

Eugene

Good Morning

What role are you playing today? During this time of pandemic response do you think you are playing a solo? Maybe not?

- **It takes generosity to discover the whole through others. If you realize you are only a violin, you can open yourself up to the world by playing your role in the concert. – Jacques Yves Cousteau**

Shakespeare wrote that, "all the world's a stage and the men and women merely players". Yes, indeed, we all have our parts to play but I think Mr. Cousteau is reaching for something deeper. What I think Mr. Cousteau is getting at is the fact that it takes a certain attitude, a generosity of spirt, to realize that your part in things matters a great deal. The violin can only do so much as a solo instrument but think of the beauty that can be created when it is joined with other stringed instruments: the woodwinds, and the brass, and the percussion. An entire symphony can leap off the page. Think of the cacophony that would result if everyone just played their own but with different sheet music. Individually, each instrument might be making very beautiful music, but when put together without the same music, without a common goal, the results can be less than desirable.

So it is with each individual. All our skills and gifts when joined with a generosity of spirit add so much to life, to the creation of a more just, inclusive and compassionate world. The opportunity to open up our "instrument" and be part of that great concert is *now*.

How will you be playing your instrument today?

Joining you in the concert.

Eugene

Good Morning

I can recall growing up and being asked by my parents to do some task and sometimes the response was, "Do I gotta?" The inference being, do I *really have* to do it? The response from my parents was usually, *Yes*!

- **A task becomes a duty from the moment you suspect it to be an essential part of that integrity which alone entitles a man to assume responsibility. – Dag Hammarskjold**

There is a lot to unpack here, but what I think Mr. Hammarskjold is getting at is, at what point do we stop doing something out of simple obligation? Something that we *have* to do and start doing it because our conscience compels us to do it. It's at this point that something transforms from being simply a task to get through, to a duty or something on a higher plane.

I am thinking that many things during this time of pandemic response and social change have moved from task to duty. Many things that we may have thought of as simply social niceties have become very vital and important to help us navigate this time in our lives. Things like consciously reaching out to others, making our voices heard on behalf of those whose voices have not been heard, remembering and affirming the basic humanity and dignity of us all.

We have a chance now, in this moment to truly understand and internalize what is our fundamental duty to each other. Those duties, along with a generosity of spirit will become the foundation stones of a more just, inclusive and compassionate society. We have a chance now, in this moment, to take those duties and as Mr. Hammarskjold says, make it an essential part of our personal integrity. This is a bold step because once we have done that, there is no going back. To someday reject those duties would be, in some incalculable way, diminish our own personal integrity.

What new duties will you take on today?

Joined with you in your new duties.

Eugene

Good Morning

It's a soft, quiet and gentle morning at my house. There is a calm that comes over me when the light is just right through the window and all I can hear is the gentle tapping of keys on a laptop. It in these calm and gentle moments that I sometimes think I can take on the world.

- **In a gentle way, you can shake the world. – Mahatma Gandhi**

There is something to be said for being gentle. In the Old Testament, Elijah climbs Mount Horeb and does not find God in a great wind, or in an earthquake, or in fire but in a small, still voice (1 Kings 19:11-13). Both Elijah and Mr. Gandhi knew the power of being gentle.

In our society, gentleness is not usually associated with strength or importance or power. What Mr. Gandhi and Elijah both grasp is that real change, permanent change, is most efficacious when it is done in a gentle way, as opposed to change that is wrought through coercion and force. Sure, you can use coercion and force to bend somebody's will to yours, but have you really changed them?

Now, to be clear, I don't think Mr. Gandhi is calling on us to be pushovers. What I think he is calling us to is show, by the example of gentleness, what it means to create a just, inclusive and compassionate society. The gentle, outreached hand to break down isolation usually gets a more welcome reaction than the incessant pounding on the door. To be gentle, I think, means to admit our own vulnerabilities as well as that of other people and, in a small, deliberate, sometimes halting way, make that outreach to others that will, in time, break down isolation and usher in a new society.

How are you going to be gentle today?

Partnering with you in gently shaking the world.

Eugene

# 28 August 2020

Good Morning

It's said that in comedy, timing is everything. It's the same in baseball and maybe even in life.

- **You don't have to swing hard to hit a home run. If you got the timing, it'll go. – Yogi Berra**

Much of what we do in life has to do with timing and scheduling. We schedule meetings, appointments, and vacations. But there is also the serendipity of timing that puts us all in the right place at the right time. Like Mr. Berra says, if we got the timing or, in other words, in the right place at the right time, "it'll go."

As I am taking a week's vacation next week, I have been thinking about you and I being together in this daily email forum. I have heard from many of you that a particular message of mine came at the right place and the right time. I want to thank everyone who has provided kind and uplifting words regarding these daily messages.

The bigger question for all of us is, what do we do when we find ourselves in the right place at the right time? Do we react with a generosity of spirit to seize that opportunity to make an impact, be it big or small? Do we use that opportunity to break down isolation, to help create a more just, compassionate, and inclusive society? Are we willing to seize that opportunity to expend the effort needed to help make something better for the future? Are we letting fear and distrust and the risk of ridicule keep us from being willing to take a chance when we are in the right place at the right time?

I want to share a personal story that illustrates this. Some years ago, I was at an evening meeting, and one of the attendees needed a ride home.

Out of fatigue, or selfishness, or unwillingness to put myself out this one time, I did not quickly step up to help. I let somebody else step up. On my way home, I realized how wrong I had been, and now, if I find myself in the right place at the right time, I try and seize the opportunity to do good. Sometimes it works out, sometimes it doesn't, but at least I know in my heart, I have taken the chance to seize that opportunity.

What opportunities will you be seizing today?

Meeting you in the right place and at the right time.

Eugene

P.S. As a gentle reminder, I will be taking a week's vacation. I plan to return to the daily emails on 8 September 2020 (after the Labor Day holiday).

# SEPTEMBER 2020

Good Morning

Well, Labor Day is over, and that marks the end of summer. The leaves will change, the weather will get colder, and we are still in the midst of pandemic response, made more complicated for some with the start of a new school year. Not much there to rejoice about … or is there?

- **Rejoicing in the good fortune of others is a practice that can help us when we feel emotionally shut down and unable to connect with others. Rejoicing generates good will. – Pema Chodron**

Now more than ever, we need to find rejoice. If we pay close enough attention, we can see that good fortune is occurring all around us. The small things are what often catch me, such as the ability to go to a favorite restaurant, the chance to see the beauty in nature, the opportunity to spend time cooking, or relax in the quiet of the back yard. All these things are things to rejoice in. The opportunities we create to connect with people and hear about their victories and their good fortune makes for even more possibilities. It's crucial, now more than ever, when isolation will be on the rise, that we find ways to hear each other's stories of good fortune and rejoice in them and tell others our stories as well.

The mere fact that we can pause, reach out and rejoice in each other's stories is in itself good fortune that should be celebrated.

Whose good fortune will you be rejoicing in today?

Partnering with you in generating goodwill.

Eugene

Good Morning

The fall is fast approaching, and many people are getting their gardens ready for the winter. What is true for the garden is also true in life.

- **Learn the lesson that, if you are to do the work of a prophet, what you want is not a scepter, but a hoe. The prophet does not rise to reign, but to root out the weeds. – Saint Bernard**

It's not easy to be a prophet. Many people avoid it. The Old Testament is replete with stories of how God would call an individual to be a prophet, and they would say something akin to "can't you get somebody else?" or, in the case of Jeremiah, he ran and hid in a cave.

The times we are living in call upon us all to be prophets, to speak with a prophetic voice. The prophet's job is not to tell people's fortune, like some sort of fortune-teller, but to point to the truth, to act as a signpost for others. Each one of us has within them a truth that needs to be announced. It may not be a truth that is revealed with words but proclaimed through the way one lives. Each one of us has a responsibility to point to the truth that will lead to a more just, inclusive, and compassionate world; a world that breaks down isolation. The ability to act as a prophet takes courage. The more we do it together, the easier the task may become.

How will you speak with a prophetic voice today?

Side by side with you as we hoe in the garden.

Eugene

Good Morning

Elvis Presley had great success with a song called *Don't Be Cruel*. There is more to being not cruel than meets the eye or expressed in Elvis' music.

- **Cruelty towards others is always also cruelty towards ourselves. – Paul Tillich**

In this time, self-care is of the utmost importance. With the colder weather starting to set in, we will be huddled up in our homes even more. We all must eat well, get plenty of rest, stay well hydrated and, maybe most importantly, find ways to keep the mind engaged, not just with the needs of work and everyday home-life, but with things that can lift the spirit and enlighten the mind.

So what does any of this have to do with being cruel? I am convinced that failure to take care of ourselves is a form of cruelty. If we are cruel to ourselves, how can we be present to others? How will we ever create a more compassionate, more inclusive, and more inclusive world? If we are not taking care of ourselves, everything we try to do for others will be just busywork.

How will you be kind to yourself today?

Partnering with you in taking care of ourselves.

Eugene

# 11 September 2020

Good Morning

Today is September 11th. This day cannot pass without some reflection on the terrible events that occurred nineteen years ago. Much will be written, said, and posted on social media about those events today. it is good to reflect on the thoughts of a simple Franciscan Friar, who, according to the New York Medical Examiner, was Victim 0001.

- **If you descent into somebody else's private hell and stand there with them, it ceases to be hell - Father Mychal Judge, OFM**

No doubt Father Judge descended, as Dante might put it, into hell on that September morning as he entered the towers. His life before September 11 dealt a great deal with suffering and entering into other's private hell. He had his hell to deal with, having been a recovering alcoholic for over 20 years and struggling with his sexual orientation in a climate and community that was not as accepting as it should be.

I think what Father Judge might want us to take from his life is the need to enter into somebody else's private hell and, maybe, more importantly, the victory that can be gained from doing that. Every time we chose to enter into somebody's private hell, we break the bonds of isolation, which is a hell in and of itself. Every time we allow somebody to enter our private hell, we begin to conquer that hell. It is the courage in ways both large and small, or as I often phrase it, the courage of the small hours, that beckons to us to reach out and break the bonds of somebody's private hell. By constantly breaking those bonds, it will lead us to a more inclusive, just and compassionate society.

Whose private hell will you be entering into today?

Standing with you in breaking bonds.

Eugene

Good Morning

I've been thinking about these messages over the weekend, and I think that maybe they have been a little on the heavy/deep side. Perhaps today, I'll start a new week by simply reminding people to be happy!

- **Whoever is happy will make others happy too. – Anne Frank**

I don't know if Anne Frank and Viktor Frankel ever crossed paths, but from this quote, it seems that at least their spirits did. I always find it amazing that, in the desperate situation that Miss Frank and Dr. Frankel found themselves in, they created a mental and spiritual space to contemplate happiness. It's all a matter of perspective and attitude.

Now, let's face facts. There is a lot right now that we probably aren't too happy about, such as the prolonged COVID-19 pandemic response, the slow pace of change in our society, the growing political rancor. All that being said, I would submit to you that each one of us, if we look hard enough, will find something that will make us happy: a home-cooked meal, some fresh baked cookies just out of the oven, some uplifting music, or a good read. It's going to take some effort. Most things that make us happy usually do. Maybe the impetus to find something that makes us happy is the knowledge of the knock-on effect. If we can be even just a little bit happy, others might be as well.

Who will you impact today with your happiness?

Joined with you in being happy today.

Eugene

Good Morning

There is an old saying that it is better to light one candle than to curse the darkness. Let's burn some candles today.

- **Thousands of candles can be lighted from a single candle, and the life of the candle will not be shortened. Happiness never decreases by being shared. – Buddha**

The use of a single candle as a metaphor for happiness is interesting. A single candle does not give off much light or heat. Perhaps that's the same thing with our happiness. It doesn't need to be a roaring fire of happiness; just something small that we can share. I've mentioned this one, and maybe it bears repeating, that much in life amounts to just showing up, being present to others. All it takes is for us to show up with our little candle of happiness.

Like I said yesterday, there is a lot to be unhappy about. Maybe all we need to do when we can't find something to be happy about is to find somebody who has "shown up" with their happiness, be it large or small. All those little happy things that we bring or get from others will cause many candles to be lighted. It is then that we, together, as we break down isolation, as we work to build a more just, inclusive, and compassionate society, will create a warming fire of happiness that all will see.

How will you be lighting your candle today?

Joined with you in increasing happiness.

Eugene

Good Morning

I think part of being happy or content has a lot to do with how we consider ourselves in relation to our past and our future.

- **I am not a has-been. I am a will be. – Lauren Bacall**

Ms. Bacall's life is indeed an interesting one. During Hollywood's golden era, she came into her own, was married to Humphrey Bogart, and made several successful films with him. Even after she was widowed, she continued to work long after many of her contemporaries had packed it in. Perhaps she had such staying power because she seemed to consider herself a work in progress.

Perhaps that is part of the key to happiness. Thinking about who we are as a work in progress, as a "great becoming," turns every day into a challenge, an adventure. Now, let's face it, some days are more of a challenge than an adventure, but that's just how the cards are dealt. Some days we go through like a fast cheetah on the Serengeti, and other days, it's like we are trying to swim in a pool of molasses. In either case, though, there is a motion; a moving forward towards what I learned in business school, a "to be condition." The key is to make every move forward a move to a more just, inclusive, and compassionate society; a move towards the breakdown of the isolation between people caused by this pandemic and the social change surrounding us.

As we continue to move forward to a "will be," it's essential that we try and bring others with us. If we are truly honest with ourselves, none of us gets to be a "will be" in isolation. People help us along the way, and in turn, we help others as they become their "will be."

Who will you be accompanying on your "will be" journey?

Partnering with you in being a "will be."

Eugene

# 17 September 2020

Good Morning

We all have ideas of what constitutes courage. Often, it has something to do with the action that can be seen. But what about the courage from within?

- **Most of us have far more courage than we ever dreamed we possessed. – Dale Carnegie**

We all know people for whom we say about, "When the chips are down, you can always rely on so and so." Who are those people in your life? How did they get such a reputation? I'm guessing that these people in our lives didn't just suddenly burst on the scene with all this courage. It's something they developed as a way of life. Part of being courageous is being secure in yourself; as a person, in your values, and your inherent value as a human being.

We also know that people can easily fake courage. Some rely on what is commonly called "liquid courage" or replace bluster and braggadocio for courage. I always like to think about courage as something developed in what I have called before "the small hours." Courage is tested when you are alone in your thoughts or maybe even alone in a stand that you take.

Courage must not be confused with force or violence. The courage I speak of is to stand on one's convictions; the courage to have the difficult conversation, the courage to be alone. That's the courage that is needed from all of us at this time.

Some people like to rely on the adage, "fake it till you make it," but I am convinced that the kind of courage I am speaking about can't, or shouldn't, be faked. No doubt it will take time, no doubt there will be some hard knocks along the way, but I believe, as Mr. Carnegie does, that we all have an untapped well of courage. All it takes is for us to find it in ourselves to drill into that well. The drilling itself is an act of courage, but I am convinced that for each of us, tapping into that well of courage and joining with others of goodwill, can create a more compassionate, just, and inclusive society.

How will you tap into your well of courage today?

United with you in the courage of the small hours.

Eugene

# 18 September 2020

Good Afternoon

It's close to the end of the day. This is probably the latest, in terms of the time of day, that I have written one of these messages, and it has given me pause to consider the fact that life is indeed worth living, even at the end of a tough day, if only we have a little bit of faith in the fact we can create that reality.

- **Believe that life is worth living and your belief will help create the fact. – William James**

I am always amazed at the strength of belief; in the power of one's own will to create a new reality for themselves. I work in a law firm where facts are paramount. If anyone goes around "creating" facts, they are in line for some serious trouble. I think what Mr. James is speaking of here is not the fabrication of facts, but how through the creative and transformative power of one's own will and belief, life can become something worth living and not just survived or put up with. It's the creation of a new reality, born out of experience, sweat, triumphs, defeats, and not unlikely, quite a few tears.

If we are to start creating a more just, compassionate, and inclusive society, we have to start by shoring up our own belief that life is indeed worth living. If we don't believe that as the bedrock upon which we will build a new society, all the lofty words and actions by others will simply be busywork.

How will you show that life is indeed worth living?

Laboring with you in creating that new fact.

Eugene

Good Morning

We are mourning the loss of a titan in the legal community. Justice Ruth Bader Ginsburg's example of the power to persuade and how to go about it is handy for these troubled times.

- **Reacting in anger or annoyance will not advance one's ability to persuade. – Ruth Bader Ginsburg**

How often do we (read: me) let our anger, annoyance, or contempt inhibit us from thinking and speaking logically and clearly about the issues we are passionate about? Justice Ginsburg understood that the message must never get confused with the messenger or how it is delivered. If anyone who disagrees with us sees anger and annoyance, the message's content and the ability to convince that person is diminished or eliminated.

I don't think that Justice Ginsburg is asking for us not to be passionate. I believe she is calling on us to channel that passion into expressions that will have the most impact. The fact that we are passionate about something can only enhance our ability to persuade. I would submit that passion is precisely what is needed if we are ever to build a more just, inclusive, and compassionate society. Such a society, full of passion for justice, is just the sort of legacy that I think would be fitting to the memory of Justice Ginsburg.

How will you honor Justice Ginsburg's life and legacy today?

Joined with you in passionate concern for others.

Eugene

Good Morning

Let's have more wisdom from Justice Ruth Bader Ginsburg. A tradition, based somewhat on the Talmud, says that if a person dies on Rosh Hashana, they are considered *tzadik*, or righteous. I think Justice Ginsburg would fit that no matter when she died.

- **Fight for the things that you care about, but do it in a way that will lead others to join you. – Ruth Bader Ginsburg**

How often do we see and hear, in the popular media, people trying to persuade others by simply decrying that the other person is wrong and that they have all the wisdom and righteousness tied up in a little blue box? If you want to be a part of the group, you have to admit you were totally wrong (and by the way, you will be continuously reminded about it), and once you have shown significant repentance, you can join the group. People who behave this way then wonder why nobody wants to join their little club.

In the marketplace of ideas, the art of persuasion is essential, and those that have mastered it always seem to find a way for people to come around to a particular way of thinking or behaving not by beating them over the head, but by giving them the space to work things out in their own way. It takes patience and kindness, but in that way, people buy in more fully.

I am reminded of an article written by Father Matt Malone, SJ, and Rev John C. Danforth (a former senator and ambassador) published on September 3, 2020, in the *Wall Street Journal*. They said, "No opinion, however passionately held, can ultimately be called truthful if it isn't spoken in charity." This is exactly the sentiment that Justice Ginsburg espoused. We are going to have to learn to speak to each other with greater charity if we are ever to build a more just, inclusive, and compassionate society. We owe this to ourselves, our future generations, and the legacy of the men and women of great wisdom and compassion. Justice Ginsburg has now joined that company.

Who and how will you lead others to join you?

Speaking with you and others in charity.

Eugene

# 23 September 2020

Good Morning

Justice Ruth Bader Ginsburg was known for her dissents. I think there is something we can learn from her attitude about dissents.

- **So that's the dissenter's hope: that they are writing not for today but for tomorrow. – Ruth Bader Ginsburg**

There is something to be said about taking the long view on things, whether it is a dissenting Supreme Court opinion, or actions we take in our own lives. How will what we say, do or write today be seen and thought about in the future? I'm sure it's a great feeling to have the immediate satisfaction of knowing we are right. It's another thing altogether to have the patience and courage to hope that, while we may not be in the majority today, we may not be with the "in" crowd now, the verdict of history will eventually come around and validate us.

It's not an easy thing to be the dissenter. As I've said before, being a prophet is no trivial task. I am convinced that now, more than ever, we need that dissenting, often prophetic voice.

If we are ever going to have any hope of building a more just, inclusive, and compassionate society, we need to look to the voice who may now be saying things that are unpopular; voices that will stir us from our places of comfort, the prophetic voices. Those voices are all around us. Maybe we are one of those voices. Perhaps we need to *become* one of those voices. Those voices can add so much to the tapestry that is our lives. We will be doing ourselves and history a disservice to ignore those voices.

What will you be saying, doing, or writing for tomorrow?

Joined with you in the dissenter's hope.

Eugene

Good Morning

We've come to the end of another week. As the seasons change and we start spending even more time indoors, it might be useful to reflect on what we might want to do as we continue to shelter in place.

- **Every day we should hear at least one little song, read one good poem, see one exquisite picture, and, if possible, speak a few sensible words. – Johann Wolfgang von Goethe**

Interestingly, Goethe is calling us to do several things, but only one of each of them. It's like he is calling us to slowly "do" and take the time to appreciate one thing at a time. We don't have to hear a whole bunch of songs or read an entire volume of poems or look at a whole gallery of pictures. One of each is enough so long as we take the time to appreciate it.

It's also essential that we speak only a few sensible words. We don't need to deliver an entire treatise on a subject. Just a few well-chosen words may be just what is required. As we encounter colleagues, friends, neighbors, or clients, it may be that they need just a few sensible words to help them get through the day or the next hour. Maybe you need a few sensible words this weekend. I am convinced that a few well-chosen words can do so much to help break isolation, provide comfort, and validate another's basic humanity. If we can all find a way to do this every day, it will go a long way to create a more just, inclusive, and compassionate society.

No doubt, some days will be more challenging than others to speak those words or listen to that one song or look at that one picture. I would submit that on those days, it may be imperative for your mental health to do it.

What sensible words will you be speaking today?

Partnering with you in slowing down and appreciating beauty.

Eugene

Good Morning

Here we are at the start of a new week. A week with challenges, potential, and opportunities. How are we (read: me) going to capitalize on them?

- **This has always been a motto of mine: Attempt the impossible in order to improve your work. – Bette Davis**

Let's face it, we all have room for improvement. I say this from personal experience. The key to making those improvements is making an attempt, in showing up to the challenge. No doubt, some days are easier to accept the challenge than others. Some days the challenge is conquered; some days, it is not. We may learn more from the times we don't conquer the challenge, or at least not on the first try than when we do.

Right now, we have many challenges swirling around us. Many of them can seem impossible. We cannot hope to overcome them all at once, but I think Miss Davis suggests that the attempt is just as important as overcoming the challenge. Miss Davis had to surmount numerous challenges in her career, from being "box office poison" for a time to her battles with studio executive Jack Warner. Through showing up to those challenges, through attempting what many thought was the impossible, she has left a legacy and a body of work that endures to this day. We can attempt the impossible so that the work we produce for our families, our clients, and society will be better.

We may not have the opportunity to attempt the impossible in such a public way as Miss Davis, but we can make those attempts, both individually and collectively as a society. We can surmount the impossible challenges that will lead to a more just, inclusive, and compassionate world.

What impossible challenge will you be meeting today?

United with you in improving the work.

Eugene

Good Afternoon

September is nearly gone, and people with swimming pools are probably planning to get them ready for the winter. There is another kind of swim that you can take year-round.

- **You cannot swim for new horizons until you have the courage to lose sight of the shore. – William Faulkner**

I'm guessing it's been hard to think about new horizons for the past six months or so. We have been forced to shelter in place due to the pandemic or unrest in the streets. Maybe now, more than ever, it's the time to be thinking and swimming towards new horizons because, let's face it, the current shore has pretty much eroded in the sea.

Whether it's a swim across a lake or voyage across the ocean in a ship under sail, any journey on the water takes planning and thought as to what or where the destination is. All that planning can be done onshore but to have any success in the voyage, one needs to go to the sea, set a course, and head to the destination. It does not inspire confidence if the captain of a ship keeps looking back at where they came from. I think that is what Mr. Faulkner is getting at: make a plan, set a goal, and move in the direction of that goal.

The times we are living in now have called into question many things. The answer to some of those questions may require many of us to forge ahead to towards a new horizon. Undertaking such a journey alone can be overwhelming. I would submit to you that the journey will be less overwhelming, and maybe even less perilous, if we launched it together. Creating a more just, inclusive, and compassionate society is not going to be the work of one of us or a few of us. It will take all of us, looking towards that new horizon and leaving the old shore of isolation, injustice, exclusivity, and mercilessness.

What new horizon will you be swimming towards today?

Joined with you losing the sight of the old shore.

Eugene

30 September 2020

What are you working toward today?  What is motivating you today?

- **Failure comes only when we forget our ideals and objectives and principles. – Jawaharlal Nehru**

I think Mr. Nehru makes a distinction between failure and not getting the desired outcome when we try and do something.  We might get the desired outcome but have we really succeeded if we have had to abandon our ideals, objectives, and principles to get that outcome?  In other words, did we sell our souls for a specific outcome?  I think that Mr. Nehru says that, no matter the outcome, if we have had to sell our souls, that constitutes a failure.

We are living in a world that is rapidly changing around us.  Old ways of doing business, of educating and relating to others are quickly moving to new models.  As we move to these new models, we have to be thinking about the outcomes from these new models, and I think the important thing is to measure them against our own ideals, objectives, and principles.  Are we being asked to change in such a way that it will fundamentally change our value system?  Maybe the critical question to be asked is how these changes will bring about a more just, inclusive, and compassionate society.  I would submit that, with all manner of change swirling about us, the more we can think about justice, inclusion, and compassion as key principles as we make choices regarding the change going on around us, the better off we and the world will be.

What ideals and principles will you remember today?

Striving with you to avoid failure.

Eugene

# OCTOBER 2020

Good Morning

Last night my wife and I toyed with the idea of firing up the furnace, but we held off. As I look out the window, I see more and more people wearing coats and fewer and fewer people in shorts. The colder weather is beginning to set in. What about the coldness between individuals? How do we keep that from being a permanently frozen state?

- **Constant kindness can accomplish much. As the sun makes ice melt, kindness causes misunderstanding, mistrust, and hostility to evaporate. – Albert Schweitzer**

On my honeymoon at Lake Louise in the Canadian Rockies, I remember a large glacier that fed Lake Louise and the minerals in the water that ran off the glacier, giving the lake a beautiful blue tint.

I think there is something to be learned from this. It is the constant presence of the sun that keeps the water coming into Lake Louise. The winters can always be rugged in the Canadian Rockies, but the sun continues to make its presence felt, even still.

Maybe that is what Dr. Schweitzer is getting at. As I have said in the past, it's easier to be kind and compassionate when the going is not so tough. Still, we must think and act with sustained kindness when the going is rough, like it is now. I would submit that those among us who are having a more challenging time, and may not be the most pleasant, are maybe the people in more dire need of some sustained kindness.

Acting out of sustained kindness and compassion is what is going to make the difference. Even when it is difficult to, our kindness's constancy will lead to a more just, compassionate, and inclusive society.

How will you show sustained kindness today?

Working with you in making the ice melt.

Eugene

# 2 October 2020

Good Afternoon

I've heard people say, and I have even said it myself, that "I got my own problems." Maybe it's time to rethink that attitude.

- **We are strong enough to bear the misfortunes of others – Francois de La Rochefoucauld**

The first thing that is interesting about Monsieur Rochefoucauld's statement is that it is definitive. He doesn't say we *may* or *we should* or *we might* be strong enough to bear others' misfortunes; he says we *are*. For me, that statement shows a lot of guts.

But what are the implications of such a statement? One must be very secure in their own identity and self-worth to muster the internal strength to be a resource to somebody in distress.

There is an old saying that a bad beating either breaks the stick or the student in the school of life. I am convinced that anyone reading these words is not broken, not by a long shot. It's the end of the week, and many of us may be pretty tired from the grind, but I am also convinced that each one of us has an untapped potential; an untapped potential to do good, to break down isolation and bring about in some way a more just, inclusive and compassionate world. The question is, will we chose to tap that potential?

I've said it before that the times we live in will be the rise and fall of many. I think that those who can rise will be those that can draw upon their own strength to reach out and help others.

How will you help bear the misfortunes of somebody else today?

Standing upright with you in breaking the stick.

Eugene

Good Morning

We are starting a new week, and I would venture a guess that many of us are still moving about, both personally and professionally, with a good deal of doubt. The question is, what do we do with it?

- **Isn't it the moment of most profound doubt that gives birth to new certainties? Perhaps hopelessness is the very soil that nourishes human hope; perhaps one could never find sense in life without first experiencing its absurdity. – Vaclav Havel**

When I was in graduate school, I took a class on creativity. One of the techniques that I learned to help foster creativity was to look at a problem or issue and start considering it by looking at it from its opposite. In other words, you consider something, and instead of thinking about what it is or what the solution would be, you think about what the solution would *not* look like (thank you, Dr. Lisa Gundry, for teaching that technique).

I think that is what Mr. Havel is calling us to do. Maybe it is the aridity of the current situation that is forcing us to think in different ways, to be creative, to consider the fact that the only way we are going to get through this pandemic or build a society that is more just, inclusive, and compassionate is by doing the hard work of tilling the soil of hopelessness together. It is out of that united effort of tilling that soil, in breaking up the hard clumps of earth that we will be able to prepare to sow good see that, as the New Testament teaches, will yield "a hundred, sixty or thirty times what was sown." (Matthew 13:8).

Mr. Havel also talks about the absurdity of life. I am quite convinced that maintaining a decent sense of humor in all this is what is going to keep us all sane. The ability for all of us together to laugh at the absurdity of our various situations is the first step towards giving birth to new certainties.

What new certainties will you be giving birth to today?

Toiling with you in tilling the soil that nourishes human hope.

Eugene

Good Morning

We all have limitations … or do we?

- **You must do the things you think you cannot do. – Eleanor Roosevelt**

Eleanor Roosevelt is an excellent example of a person overcoming difficulties. Even though she was born into a privileged life, her own shyness and the fact that she was a woman were significant limitations. Still, history shows how she became Franklin Roosevelt's legs after he was diagnosed with polio. She was able to go where he could not go and say what he could not say. Arguably, she could be considered one of the great women of the 20th Century.

But what about us? Most of us don't have access to the power or influence that Eleanor Roosevelt did … or do we? When I consider this, I always come back to two ideas: creativity and personal agency.

The time is now for each of us to draw on the store of creativity that we all possess and use our agency to come to terms with the problems of our time. No one person has all the answers, but the choice is now staring us in the face. Are we going to use our creativity, agency, and privilege to break down the isolation this pandemic has forced us into and help create a more just, inclusive, and compassionate world?

I am convinced that each creative act, no matter how small, each expenditure of personal agency and privilege on behalf of others, will have an impact. We can't just sit by and wait for somebody else to act. In every act of compassion that we show, we are doing something that nobody else in that time and place can do.

What thing will you do today that you thought you could not do?

Joined with you in creative personal agency.

Eugene

Good Morning

There is an old saying that it is easier to ask for forgiveness than to ask for permission. There is some wisdom in that, and maybe because of it, it is better to take a risk.

- **He who risks and fails can be forgiven. He who never risks and never fails is a failure in his whole being. – Paul Tillich**

The question that faces all of us is, do we risk it or we play it safe? It's easy to use this time of sheltering in place to sit and wait everything out simply. I also think there is a difference between taking a risk and being foolhardy. We have so many opportunities (also known as risks) we can capitalize on at this time. We also have to consider what we are willing to risk our personal capital on.

When taking a risk, there is always the calculus of what is the return. Maybe we should also make the calculus if we don't take the risk.

In some shape or fashion, I am convinced that we need to be taking risks to break down isolation between people and be the salve on the wounds, both old and new, in the hearts of many. We need to be taking risks to help usher in a more just, compassionate, and inclusive society. If we take these risks, there is always a chance of being rejected, of motives being questioned, of unintended consequences, but here again, the calculus of what our world would be like if we didn't take the risk must be considered.

In life, not everything is black and white; there is a lot of grey, and that is part of what we deal with when we decide if we are going to take a risk, especially if it a risk of an interpersonal nature. The outcomes may not be evident. Maybe the best judge of success or failure, when we risk, is how we feel when we look in the mirror the morning after. If when we do that we can say we would do it again, then no matter what, chances are we won't have to ask for forgiveness.

What risks will you be taking today.

United with you in never being a failure.

Eugene

# 8 October 2020

Good Morning

We've all been taught that it's polite to say please and thank you. Maybe these social graces are more than just polite niceties but something more fundamental.

- **Gratitude is not only the greatest of virtues, but the parent of all the others. – Marcus Tullius Cicero**

This is a tough time for many; there is an ongoing pandemic, needed social change, economic and political insecurity. So what do we have to be thankful for? Maybe gratitude doesn't spring from an ability to simply rattle off a list of things we are grateful for, but from an attitude; a way of looking at life, so to speak.

I think that how we look at each other is one place to start. Are we looking at each other as somebody endowed with grace and beauty, as someone with their own unique story that should be celebrated? Or have current conditions caused us to be jaded in our view of others, to view others with suspicion? I have the notion that any attempt we as individuals make in terms of breaking down isolation, of healing divisions amongst people, of creating a more just, inclusive, and compassionate society must be grounded in the idea (or ideal) that "the other" is not a being that is to be rescued or pitied but a person, not much different than us, with their own value and dignity and someone we should be grateful for. Anything less, and I think we are just doing busywork with no lasting impact.

Now, with all that being said, I know there are individuals in each of our lives that are difficult to be grateful for. It may not be wise or healthy to suddenly feel the need to be chummy with them. Maybe it's enough for us to say of them, "They mean well, God love them" (that's a very popular phrase in my wife's family). Maybe if we can do that with those difficult individuals, it might lead to a more significant wellspring of gratitude and a fountain of other virtues.

Who will you be grateful for today?

In gratitude for you and with you.

Eugene

Good Morning

I remember going into a car dealership, and at one point during the negotiations, the salesman says something to the effect of "here's the deal, take it or leave it," but are those our only options in life?

- **The world is before you and you need not take it or leave it as it was when you came in. – James Baldwin**

I remember years ago, visiting the United Nations building in New York and was struck by the statute of a man hitting a sword and turning it into a plow. The imagery is striking, and the message is clear: we all have the power to make a positive change in the world. We don't have to just take it as is or walk away.

Not only do I think Mr. Baldwin is showing us a "third way," but he is also throwing down a challenge. It seems to me he is saying, "You don't like how things are? What are you going to do about it?" No doubt Mr. Baldwin took up that challenge a lot during his lifetime.

So, how are we going to respond to the challenges of our own time? Are we going to retreat into tribalism, or will we make the moves needed to help bring about a more just, inclusive, and compassionate society?

Every day we are confronted with this choice. We can move in the direction of change or accept things as they are and simply walk away. Granted, some days will be more challenging than others to move in the direction of change. Some days, it will feel like you are moving backward. I am convinced that, when we feel we are not moving forward, there will be somebody else to "take up the slack" and help move things forward on those days. That's why I feel it is so vital that we take the time to break down the isolation we are experiencing now. We are all going to be needed to keep things moving forward. Some of us can make big changes, others can make small changes, but big or small, we are all needed.

What choices will you be making today?

Working with you towards the third way.

Eugene

Good Morning

There is a common phrase in Italian to refer to a good person: *una persona di prima classe*. The literal translation is "a first-class person." Here in the US, we have a comparable phrase, which is "a stand-up guy" or a "stand-up person." How do we get there? Maybe the path to being a stand-up person is authenticity.

- **Always be a first-rate version of yourself, instead of a second-rate version of somebody else. – Judy Garland**

I remember working at a previous firm, and when word got out that I was moving to a different firm, one of the partners in the firm expressed regret at my leaving because I was one of the few people "who knows what he is doing." I always held this person in great esteem, and it was a pleasure to receive such a compliment.

I have been pondering on how one really gets to a point in one's life where they really know what they are doing, whether at work, at home, or in the world in general. I've concluded that authenticity is the key to excellence in anything one does. If one is really true to themselves, that becomes part and parcel of everything they do: whether it's the carpenter who is building a house, an attorney trying a case or putting a deal together, the doctor or nurse in the ER, the cop on the beat, or the clergyman in the pulpit.

We owe it to ourselves, our families, and society as a whole to be a first-rate version of ourselves. Our world can be transformed into a more just, inclusive, and compassionate world only by people who are true to themselves at the most basic level.

How will you be a first-rate person today?

Working with you in avoiding the second rate.

Eugene

Good Morning

I remember years ago, there was a religious program on Sunday mornings called *The Hour of Power*. Maybe we need to start thinking about The Hour of Grace.

- **For me, every hour is grace. And I feel gratitude in my heart each time I can meet someone and look at his or her smile. – Elie Wiesel**

I had the time last evening to watch a young Franciscan friar give a YouTube talk about "returning to normal." The thrust of his comments was that he was sick of hearing about returning to normal because he was convinced that 1) the normal that we left wasn't that great in many respects and 2) there is no going back to those old ways of behaving and relating to each other.

I think Mr. Wiesel is giving us a blueprint to help us map our way forward. Maybe now is the time, when we are cut off from each other due to social distancing, to really appreciate those times we are with others; be it our own families or the people we meet at the grocery store or who pass by as we look out the window. Every smile we share, every kind word given, and every comfort we can express is an act of defiance. It is an act that is rejecting the old way of looking upon "the other" with suspicion and antipathy.

Each one of those encounters is an opportunity for grace and gratitude. I'm thinking that looking at others as vehicles of grace and gratitude will do much to help usher in a new world of compassion, inclusion, and justice.

For whom will you be grace for today?

Greeting you with a smile.

Eugene

# 14 October 2020

Good Morning

I remember as a young boy getting asked the question, in a rather nasty tone, "Hey kid, what are you looking at?". My typical repost, especially if I was feeling particularly snarky, was usually, "Not much!". Maybe the bigger question is not what we are looking at, but what we are focused on.

- **Your destiny is to fulfill those things upon which you focus most intently. So choose to keep your focus on that which is truly magnificent, beautiful, uplifting and joyful. Your life is always moving toward something. – Ralph Marston**

Focus, as Mr. Marston implies, requires a certain amount of intensity. I remember watching the movie *The Karate Kid* and Mr. Miyagi always insisting on Daniel's (his young student) focus and concentration.

The question for us now and in the future is, what are we choosing to focus on? It would be the easy thing to do to focus on what is wrong, unjust, or not inclusive in our world. The more significant challenge is for us to change our own focus and on a larger scale, changing the focus of those we come in contact with. Mr. Marston makes a direct line between fulfilling one's destiny and where is the center of one's focus. To move towards what is magnificent, beautiful, uplifting, and joyful is a choice that we have to make every day. Some days, it's harder to do than others. Some days, we can bring others along, some days, others bring us along, some days we have to go it alone.

The choices we make now and in the coming days on our focus will bear fruit in the future. Let's focus on those things that will lead to a more just, inclusive, and compassionate world.

How will you be changing your focus today?

Joining with you in the magnificent, beautiful, uplifting and joyful.

Eugene

Good Morning

There is lots of talk about whom is superior to whom, in politics, in social life, in economic life. I remember watching a movie where one of the characters complained about everyone "trying to be better than their betters." Maybe we need to start thinking about being superior to ourselves.

- **There is nothing noble in being superior to your fellow men. True nobility lies in being superior to your former self. – Ernest Hemingway**

There is an old saying about the unexamined life not being worth living. There is a tremendous amount of truth in that. Every day has the potential of being "a great becoming" in that we have the chance every day to be and become truly noble by looking within and asking ourselves, "What can I do a little bit better today?" As you know, I am a big believer in the fact that everybody can do something. It doesn't have to be something huge. All it takes is the extra smile you share with somebody, the extra minute you take before you utter that sharp word, the bottle of water you offer to the postal worker at your door. I think this is what Mr. Hemingway is getting at. All these small acts of kindness and consideration, compassion, justice, and inclusion make up true nobility.

Interestingly, Mr. Hemingway uses the term nobility. Here in the United States, we arguably don't have a great tradition of a noble class like there is in other parts of the world. In this country, we have a long history with class, usually based on economics. I think Mr. Hemingway uses the idea of nobility because it can transcend economics and class. I have seen true nobility in the eyes of those at the lowest rungs of the economic ladder and a lack of nobility by people of great wealth. Each one of us has the opportunity to be and become truly noble by the choices we make, how we decide to improve ourselves and the effort we are willing to make to help create a more just, inclusive, and compassionate society.

How are you going to be superior to your former self today?

Journeying with you in the quest for true nobility.

Eugene

Good Morning

There is an old saying about making do with what you have. Are we called to just make do, or are we called to flourish?

- **The measure of who we are is what we do with what we have. – Vince Lombardi**

To me, there seems to be a certain sense of resignation in the old adage about making do. To me, it seems to come from a perspective or attitude of scarcity and not of abundance. I think that Coach Lombardi is trying to turn that on its head. He seems to be saying that people will judge us based on what we do with what we have, and consequently, we need to try and go beyond just "making do."

The past seven months have been a challenge for all of us. We have been forced to make do with social distancing and Zoom meetings instead of meeting in person. We have been forced to make do with going to "virtual worship" instead of going to our church, temple, mosque, or synagogue. We have been forced to make do with changes in how we celebrate key life events.

Maybe now is the time to take stock of what Coach Lombardi is challenging us to do. I am convinced that there is an untapped well of creativity in each of us. That creativity is what will make us move from an attitude of scarcity to a mindset of abundance, from simply making do to flourishing. I am also convinced that we won't be able to flourish every day all the time. All it takes is for one thing we do on any particular day to flourish to move us from scarcity to abundance.

What will you do today that will flourish?

Moving with you from scarcity to abundance.

Eugene

Good Morning

There is something called the "month's mind" in the Roman Catholic tradition, which is a requiem mass celebrated about a month after a person dies. Maybe it's good to reflect on the wisdom these two individuals who have recently died, both giants in their respective fields.

- **There comes a time when you have to stand up and be counted. – Gale Sayers**

- **When a thoughtless or unkind word is spoken, best tune out. – Ruth Bader Ginsberg**

I don't know if Mr. Sayers and Justice Ginsberg ever met, but I am sure they had to put into practice what the other person said. But what are the implications for us? What can we learn from their wisdom?

We have heard so much in recent days about getting involved and making your voice heard, whether in a political context or an interpersonal context. I am convinced that standing up and being counted is not an excuse to fall into tribalism, nor is it license just to shout somebody else down. This challenging time in world history is calling upon all of us, in ways great and small, to stand up and be counted for things like justice, inclusion, and compassion. It takes plenty of guts to do that when often, the attitude is, as the late Mike Royko put it, "Ubi Est Mea" which, when translated is rendered, "Where's mine?"

When one stands up to be counted, one is by definition making themselves a target. No doubt Mr. Sayers was a target for a lot of unpleasantness and hostility because of who he was and his friendship with his roommate Brian Piccolo. I'm guessing that Mr. Sayers had to tune out a lot of unpleasantness.

Here is perhaps where Mr. Sayers' and Justice Ginsberg's wisdom comes together. In rejecting and tuning out the voices of division, exclusion, injustice, and indifference, we are, in essence, standing up to be counted.

More often than not, when we stand up in such a way, we'll find that we are not standing alone.

How will you stand up to be counted today?

United with you in tuning out the voices of injustice and indifference.

Eugene

# 20 October 2020

Good Morning

Every day is a busy day. It seems that we always have one more thing to do. Maybe it's time to think about having one less thing, but not in the way you might think.

- **Lieutenant Dan got me invested in some kind of fruit company. So then I got a call from him, saying we don't have to worry about money no more. And I said, that's good! One less thing. – Forrest Gump, as spoken by Tom Hanks in the movie *Forrest Gump***

I've always thought that is the best line in that movie. It speaks to a simplicity of spirit and of heart; an ability to see what is essential. It also has an optimistic tone to it. Here is this simple person, and all of a sudden, he has great wealth, and instead of thinking of all the issues that go along with it, all he says is that it's one less thing to worry about.

What can we do to have one less thing? I don't think it has anything to do with ticking things off a to-do list. Maybe what we need to be thinking about in terms of one less thing is how we can help one less person feel less isolated; one less person release that their voice and story has merit.

There is no getting around that the winter coming, at least in the northern hemispheres, will be colder and longer because of the prolonged isolations we are all experiencing. We owe it to our fellow travelers on this planet and ourselves to take this time and try and make one less person feel isolated, unheard, unvalued and discounted. I firmly believe that helping make one less person feel this way is a better use of our time than simply ticking something off a to-do list.

Maybe the to-do list needs to be rethought not as tasks to do but people to connect with.

What will be your one less thing today?

Partnering with you in rethinking the to-do list and what should be on it.

Eugene

Good Morning

How many people watch the Superbowl simply for the ads? How much post-game discussion is centered on the ads? I think there is a lesson in that, and it comes from arguably American most renowned advertising executive.

- **We want consumers to say, 'That's a hell of a product' instead of, 'That's a hell of an ad.' – Leo Burnett**

Many people (read: me) get so involved in what I will call the packaging of life. We (read: me) spend many hours honing our LinkedIn profile or our social media presence. We spend a lot of time on material goods, or what I might call the advertising of life. Now before I go any further, I want to say that I am *not* advocating that everyone sell all they have and live in a cave. Material goods are necessary to help sustain human existence.

The question becomes, what do need to move beyond simply sustaining to flourishing? Yes, even in this time of pandemic response, social change, and political uncertainty, it is possible to flourish and not at the expense of another person.

Flourishing can take many forms, but it takes work. We can flourish physically, but that means getting up every morning to exercise (ugh). We can flourish in the life of the mind, but that means reading and taking time to think and write. Perhaps this is the time we can flourish in our relationships, but this means we need to take the time to reach out in solidarity with others, to break down isolation, to challenge the barriers of race and class that over time have built up between people. It means transforming "the product" of our lives into one that can help usher in a society of justice, inclusion and compassion. These tasks are by no means easy or without setbacks, but that's what it takes to move beyond the "advertisement" to a flourishing life.

Will you be working on "the product" or "the ad" today?

Striving with you towards a flourishing life.

Eugene

Good Afternoon

What does it take to be truly free? Is open revolt with arms the only way?

- **The only way to deal with an unfree world is to become so absolutely free that your very existence is an act of rebellion. – Albert Camus**

We who live in the West, and especially the United States, like to think we live in a totally free society. We like to think that we can think and act as we please. The reality, though, is we often live in a state of little or no freedom. We are restricted by our economic situation, our educational situation, our social situation, and many other limits that are put on us. Maybe the only true freedom lies in the space between our ears. Perhaps that is what Monsieur Camus is trying to tell us.

The question now becomes how do we gain that freedom? Maybe that freedom is achieved by the shedding of prejudices, of old hurts and grudges. It can also be achieved in the constant affirmation of the fundamental dignity of ourselves and others. Real freedom for ourselves is what happens when we find the strength to reach out to others to help create a more just, inclusive, and compassionate society. I would submit that those small acts of compassion we show to each other in this time of pandemic response, social change and political uncertainty are the acts of rebellion that Monsieur Camus is speaking about. Our ability to be genuinely free and reach beyond ourselves is the rebellion against those forces that would divide and separate people.

I think that this is a cycle. The more we reach out in compassion, the more we are free, and the more we are free, the more we can rebel against the forces that would divide us, and the more significant that rebellion, the easier it becomes for others to reach out in compassion. But it has to start somewhere. It has to start with you and me.

How will your existence be an act of rebellion today?

United with you in living absolutely free.

Eugene

Good Morning

Yesterday, we considered freedom as resistance. Today, I thought it might be interesting to think about freedom as victory.

- **Freedom is never given; it is won. – A. Philip Randolph**

I think Monsieur Camus' and Mr. Randolph's perspectives on freedom are two sides of the same coin. That being said, I am pretty sure that, given Mr. Randolph's history and his work with the Pullman Porters and the civil rights movement, he may have been speaking of freedom from a political or social perspective. Still, I think his statement is equally applicable to freedom in the interior life.

Every day offers a new opportunity to free ourselves from the attitudes, ways of living, and maybe even relationships, that keep us from being the people that we truly can be and are truly called to be; people of compassion, inclusion, and justice. Every time we find a way to reach out in solidarity to others who are isolated or experience injustice, or are not included in the wider society, we score a victory. In reaching out to others, we help free others from the bonds of isolation that they are experiencing. For ourselves, we share the freedom that comes when we affirm others' inherent dignity because in doing that, we affirm our dignity and are thus made free from that which would deny us our dignity.

It goes without saying that these victories and freedoms are hard won. It is a long campaign, and it is constant. I think we as humans are constantly called to affirm our dignity and freedom and that of others. It is a voice that beckons and urges us on to the next mountain top.

What freedom will you win today?

Joined with you towards the next mountain top.

Eugene

# 26 October 2020

Good Morning

It's the start of a new work week, and many of us are feeling like life is becoming like the instructions on the shampoo bottle: "wash, rinse, repeat" or that we are all working from the same script every day ... but do we need to?

- **I don't worry too much about the script, I just ad lib, like Pearl Bailey. – Mahalia Jackson**

We all seem to be working from scripts; scripts on how to shelter in place properly, scripts for how we should (or should not) be venturing outside. This morning, I even heard of "scripts" on how to do Halloween trick-or-treating. Now, many of the scripts are needed, but we need not have our entire life scripted.

This time of pandemic response, social change, and political uncertainty might be just the impetus we need to get thinking about how we have scripted our lives. Perhaps those scripts need revising or tossing out altogether. Think of the beauty that Ms. Jackson or Ms. Bailey were able to bring about because they went off script once in a while (or maybe often). As it is with performance, so can it be with life.

Maybe we need to think about ad-libbing some of our relationships. Perhaps we can open those relationships to new vistas and experiences that will be fodder for personal growth. Maybe by thinking and acting differently in our relationships, we can break down the isolation this pandemic has forced us into. Perhaps it can help us hear those voices that we have not heard clearly or have not been permitted a full voice in our world because of our script or the role we think we have.

Going off script is never easy. One of the hardest, but often most successful, forms of comedy is improv, where there is no script. If we are to have any hope for a better tomorrow, many of us will have to go off-script.

How will you be going off script today?

Joined with you in ad-libbing to a better tomorrow.

Eugene

Good Morning

We all have dreams, or at least we had them until somebody told us to "grow up" and "be realistic." Maybe that is not the best sage advice ever given.

- **Hold fast to dreams, for if dreams die, life is a broken-winged bird that cannot fly. – Langston Hughes**

No doubt, it's getting harder to dream. We live in the middle of a pandemic, there is political uncertainty and unrest in many places in the US and, maybe more troubling, there is unrest in people's hearts. Mr. Hughes uses striking imagery about those who have lost their dreams. In nature, I think there isn't a more pitiful sight than a bird with a broken wing. Often, there is little that can be done for that bird.

But what about us? It would be the easy thing just to give in and let dreams die and try to hobble through the rest of our lives; or we can choose to reimagine a new and different future for ourselves, with new dreams to work towards and hold onto. Maybe that reimagining is what we need as the cold weather starts to close in and we become even more isolated. Not only do we owe it to ourselves to hold onto dreams, but we also need to reach out to others whose dreams have long since died. Maybe all these people need is a little encouragement from us to forge new dreams and imagine a new future for themselves. It's in forging those new dreams that we can all envision a new society; a society built on inclusion, justice, and compassion.

What new dreams will you forge today?

Supporting you as we each hold on to our dreams.

Eugene

Good Morning

With the increase of COVID-19 cases, there has been much talk about increasing restrictions to keep people safe. But what does the need for safety really entail?

- **To keep oneself safe does not mean to bury oneself. – Lucius Annaeus Seneca**

Before I go any further, I want to say that I am *not* calling on people to disregard the best practices to keep people physically safe. Please wear a mask when needed, practice social distancing, and wash your hands.

What I think Seneca is getting is at is that we should not use this time, when we need to take precautions to be physically safe, as an excuse to cut ourselves off from the community or world at large. From what I see in the news, I worry it might be easy for people to simply bury themselves until this is all over, like waiting for a bad dream to be over.

I think now, more than ever, it is incumbent upon each one of us to fight what might be an instinct to hunker down in isolation and to reach out to others in solidarity and in a rejection of the isolation that we all are enduring. It is also a good time for taking stock of who we are as individuals and what we want a new society to look like. This pandemic and the social and political changes in play make it evident that there is no "going back" to the old normal. Let's face it; there was a lot wrong with the old normal.

I'm a big advocate of doing the little things in life. The simple phone call to a relative or business associate, a text to a person you know is hurting, showing a little more patience with people we meet in the street or at the grocery, maybe even buying a gift card from a local restaurant that you know is up against it financially. I like to think that all these little acts of kindness and solidarity are one more fist shaken in the face of those forces that would divide us and those interior voices that might tell us to just "wait it out."

I remember years ago seeing a poster from the First World War where a child climbed on her father's knee, and the caption on the poster was, "What did you do in the war, Daddy?" The look on the father's face intimated that he did not have a good answer. When the next generation asks what did we do in the pandemic of 2020, will we have the same look on our faces?

What will you do to not bury yourself today?

Joined with you in doing the little things.

Eugene

Good Morning

For many of us (read: me), some days, it's just enough to get out of bed and try and get something done that day. Maybe on those days, that's all it takes to keep moving, to keep pressing on.

- **The future rewards those who press on. I don't have time to feel sorry for myself. I don't have time to complain. I'm going to press on. – Barack Obama**

I find it interesting that President Obama uses the phrase "press on". For me, that phrase conjures up several images. First, it evokes exertion; we are not just moving forward but putting some effort into our moving forward. It also evokes forward motion; we are not just moving aimlessly about but are moving with a purpose. Finally, it evokes an urgency; we need to press on, and we need to do it *now*.

No doubt there are a myriad of things that we need to press on with right now. There are the macro issues of responding to the pandemic and the social change and political uncertainty swirling about us. We need to press on with micro issues such as the care of those entrusted to us, staying productive in our professional lives, and trying to stay healthy, both physically and emotionally.

I want to believe that we are not doing all this pressing on in isolation. I feel it is incumbent on all of us to help those who need a little more effort in their own pressing on than they can give. No doubt, each one of us will come to a point at some time or another where we need the help of others in our pressing on.

I do not doubt that each of us, pressing on as we can and helping others press on, will break the isolation that this pandemic has wrought and will be the harbinger of a new world based on justice, inclusion, and compassion. Maybe that is one of the rewards President Obama is referring to.

How will you be pressing on today?

Joined with you in helping each other press on.

Eugene

# 30 October 2020

Good Morning

I have tried not to be too partisan in these daily reflections, but I have been political, but maybe not in a way some may think.

- **I have come to the conclusion that politics are too serious a matter to be left to the politicians. – Charles de Gaulle**

The Latin root of the word politics is *politicus*. One of the meanings can be construed as "of citizens," so in that way, each of these reflections is political because it concerns citizens; be they citizens of a country or the world.

It would not surprise me if General de Gaulle referred to professional politicians who run governments and make policy, but I think there is a deeper meaning that can be drawn out of this.

There are many forces arrayed who would be happy to tell us how to relate to each other. Perhaps in some way, I am doing that, although that is not my intent. What I am striving to do is to encourage all of us to rethink how we relate to each other during these times; how we take the experiences we are now going through of pandemic response, social change, and political change to reshape or create new institutions and attitudes on how we relate to each other.

If we are ever to have any chance at all, these new and changed institutions must be based on justice, inclusion, and compassion. If they are not, anything we do in planning for the future will just be busywork.

The time is now, as we move into the final weeks of 2020, a year of great difficulty, sadness, and uncertainty, to ask fundamental questions of ourselves.

How can we use this great test to forge a new society, a new way of thinking for ourselves, and a new way of relating to others, especially those relegated to life's margins?

Robert Kennedy once said, "Some men see things as they are, and ask why. I dream of things that never were and ask why not." Maybe the prophet Joel from the Old Testament said it better many years ago, "And afterward, I will pour out my Spirit on all people. Your sons and daughters will prophesy, your old men will dream dreams, your young men will see visions" (Joel 2:28).

What visions will you have today?

United with you in speaking with a prophetic voice for our future.

Eugene

# NOVEMBER 2020

Good Morning

It's the start of another week, and here in the USA, a significant week with elections on Tuesday. It's just one of many things that we can get tied up in knots about … but is it worth it?

- **You only have a few years to play this game and you can't play it if you're all tied up in knots. – Willie Stargell**

No doubt many of us are concerned, and rightly so, about the issues facing our nation and our world. We have an ongoing pandemic, social change, and political uncertainty. I think there is a fine line between being concerned and getting tied up in knots. I have this image of a knot as something firm, in place, immovable. If we allow ourselves to get tied up in knots, we'll just end up not doing anything; we'll become paralyzed and not make any contribution to society.

There is something to be learned about this from physiology. What do people do when they get a knot in a leg or arm muscle? They try to work it out; they get a massage or stretch it. The critical thing here is that they do something. They don't let the knot just sit there.

We all have a finite amount of time to "play this game" Mr. Stargell was speaking about. He was talking about baseball, but you can say the same thing about life itself. We all have a finite time, and we won't be able to do something if we allow ourselves to get tied up in knots.

Now is the time for all of us to do something. We can do something to break down isolation and help usher in a new society based on justice, compassion, and inclusion. We can work out our knots, both individually and collectively.

How will you work out your knot today?

Partnering with in stretching for a better tomorrow.

Eugene

P.S. Today is the last day for early voting in many places. Please take advantage of that! I'm not so concerned about how you will mark your ballot, but that you take the time either today or tomorrow to mark one.

Good Morning

Today is polling day in the USA. No doubt we'll see lots of red, white, and blue and appeals to patriotism. Maybe it's time we reflect on patriotism.

- **True patriotism hates injustice in its own land more than anywhere else. – Clarence Darrow**

It's easy to be a patriot when things are going well. It's harder to be a patriot when we have to shine a bright light on our national shortcomings, as Mr. Darrow seems to be advocating. Patriotism does not mean just waving a flag and shouting "USA! USA! USA!" incessantly.

True patriotism doesn't call on the very best of us to think about not how comfortable or secure we are, or how far we have come in any particular aspect of national life, but instead to think about what still needs to be done and to find ways to productively move society forward. Perhaps in this time, moving the culture forward means breaking down the isolation the current pandemic has caused.

One way to be a true patriot is to consider what we as individuals can do though collective action to bring about a society based on justice, inclusion, and compassion. No matter what our station in life is, we all have a part to play in making our society better. Playing that part the best we can is an emblem of true patriotism.

How will you be a true patriot today?

Laboring with you in building a better society.

Eugene

Good Morning

Well, it's the morning after polling day and we are still waiting for final results. It's a hard waiting; a waiting that bears down on the spirit, a waiting with no sure outcome.

- **For anything worth having one must pay the price; and the price is always work, patience, love, self-sacrifice - no paper currency, no promises to pay, but the gold of real service. – John Burroughs**

There is a lot of different kinds of waiting going on today. Some are simply waiting for election results, some are waiting for their human value to be affirmed, some are waiting for their voices to be heard, and some are simply waiting for work, bread, and dignity.

I remember watching a film based on the book by Morris West entitled *The Shoes of the Fisherman*. There is one scene where the character, played by Anthony Quinn, steps off an airplane in Rome after many years in a Soviet work camp in Siberia. He makes the following statement about work, bread, and dignity: "These things are good in themselves whether they exist in Rome or Siberia and work, bread and dignity do exist in Siberia."

I find that to be a profound statement. No matter how the results of yesterday's elections pan out, each one of us is going to have to get up tomorrow morning and ask ourselves if we are simply going to wait around for some politician to provide the answers we need, or if we are going to pay what Mr. Burroughs calls "the gold of real service". That gold includes patience and the work and self-sacrifice required to break down the isolation that this pandemic is wreaking on society; the work required to bring about a society based on justice, compassion, and inclusion that will be so strong that no political movement, no politician, will be able to topple it.

How will you pay the gold of real service today?

Seeking with you bread, work and dignity for all.

Eugene

Good Morning

There has been a lot of "taking sides" over the past few months. Many people think taking sides is not a good thing. Some people think we should just "get with the program" and forget about taking sides. Maybe we need more people taking sides.

- **We must take sides. Neutrality helps the oppressor, never the victim. Silence encourages the tormentor, never the tormented. – Elie Wiesel**

In British political life, there is a phrase used to describe the party not in power which is "the loyal opposition." Some may consider it an archaic term, but I think there is something there for us to learn from and consider as we wait out election results. This term implies that the party out of power may oppose the policies and practices of the party in power, while also remaining loyal to the underpinnings of that particular system of government, be it a constitution or monarch.

The question for us now, in this day, is, how are we going to choose to express that loyalty while still taking sides?

We can take personal and collective initiative to do things that will break down the isolation between people, which affirms others' dignity and individual agency. That fosters and encourages the voices of those whose voices have been muted or silenced to ring out in truth. In doing these things, we are, as Mr. Wiesel is saying, taking a side. In taking that side, we are loyal to those principles that will lead to the creation of a society rooted in justice, compassion, and inclusion.

No matter what happens with the election results, there will always be a need for a loyal opposition for taking sides in those things that will uplift society.

We need not wait around for election results. We can do these things and take those sides every day, no matter who is in political power or not.

How will you be taking a side today?

Laboring with you in moving away from neutrality.

Eugene

Good Morning

It's becoming more and more apparent as the vote totals come in that we are a nation of interdependent people.

- **However fragmented the world, however intense the national rivalries, it is an inexorable fact that we become more interdependent every day. – Jacques Yves Cousteau**

Monsieur Cousteau hits the nail on the head when he says that we, as human beings, are moving towards more interdependence than to strictly independence.

Now, I'm not here to debate the rightness or wrongness of how elections are run in the US, or if we should abolish the electoral college, but I think the experience of this election cycle has brought home the fact that we in this nation, and even the world, need to start thinking about each other and looking out for each other.

So the question becomes for us today: What are the implication of this growing interdependence?

The COVID-19 pandemic and its response have fundamentally altered, possibly forever, the way we interact with each other. From the need for social distancing to the Zoom call's ubiquity, we have had to adapt to new ways of relating and connecting. Whether we like or not, we will be more interdependent as a people, which means if we are going to move forward as a people, we need to start understanding others' needs and aspirations. Those who live in urban areas need to better understand those in rural areas and vice versa. The old need to consider the young's aspirations, and the young need to think about the experiences that have shaped the older members of the community. Those who have positions of privilege and power need the perspective of those who do not.

To be genuinely interdependent, we need to break down the isolation that has brought us to this place. This isolation has been many years in the making. The current pandemic has only brought it into sharper contrast.

I am convinced that if we don't take seriously the need to become interdependent, we will see election maps in the US repeating the same old blue versus red divides. I'm sure that very few of us want to relive the past election cycle.

What will you do to be more interdependent today?

Continuing on the journey with you to better understanding.

Eugene

Good Morning

It looks like we have results for the recent presidential election. The question now for all of us is what comes next?

- **My dream is of a place and a time where America will once again be seen as the last best hope of earth. – Abraham Lincoln**

I think President Lincoln's words are as applicable now as they were when he uttered them in the 1800s. The question now facing us is, how do we make this country the last best hope on earth?

I put great store in the phrase from the 146th Psalm that stated not to put your trust in princes. For better or for worse, I have become very skeptical of politicians, and I am convinced that if we are going to make President Lincoln's dream a reality, it will have to be up to each one of us. No politician's or government's program will ever match what the concerted effort of an aroused population can do.

I am not unaware of the forces arrayed against those who would make America the last best hope on earth. Some want to just "look out for number one," and so long as they are fulfilled and content, the rest is simply irrelevant.

So what would make America be the last best hope? I think Lincoln's vision would include an America based on justice, inclusion, and compassion. We've seen precious little in our discourse as a society from all aspects of these principles.

The transformation of America into the last best hope of the earth will not occur based on the outcome of an election or the implementation of a particular policy. This transformation will be accomplished by the concerted effort of Americans who want to make this transformation a reality. Our actions of outreach and compassion, especially to those with whom we may not agree or have been on the margins of society is what will make Lincoln's vision a reality.

If America is going to be the last best hope of the world, then each of us is going to have to be the first and last best hope of America.

How will you be the best hope for America today?

Tirelessly laboring with you to make Lincoln's vision a reality.

Eugene

Good Afternoon

I'm sure everyone is familiar with the phrase "having a seat at the table."
But what do you do when there is no seat for you?

- **If they don't give you a seat at the table, bring a folding chair. –
Shirley Chisholm**

There are many tables we all should be sitting at: tables at work, tables at
home, tables in the various organizations we belong. The key word here
is *should*. We should be sitting at all these tables, but sometimes, instead
of cooperation and inclusion, which should be the hallmark of all the
tables we are sitting at, exclusion is the rule.

So, where does that leave us? I think this is what Ms. Chisholm is getting
at in her comment. If nobody wants to give you a seat at the table, bring
your own chair and make a place for yourself. The act of making a place
for yourself is an act that affirms your own dignity. Also, by making a seat
for yourself at the table, you bring a richness to any discussion or
decision-making process. You bring the wisdom of your own experience
to bear.

It's not enough to make a place for yourself at the table. I would submit
that, in keeping with Ms. Chisholm's principle of bringing your own chair,
we all need to think about bringing an extra chair for those whose voices
have been muted or even excluded. In doing so, we must not act out of
pity or sympathy, but the act must be rooted in the principles of justice,
inclusion, and compassion. Anything else, in my opinion, is not
acknowledging the dignity of the other person; it can be perceived as
condescending.

Now, I will admit that there are times when there is indeed no room at
the table. What do we do then? In those cases, through concerted efforts
and valuing others' abilities and contributions, we build a new table. What
I mean by that is, if we are ever to move forward in justice, inclusion and

compassion, fundamental changes will have to happen in institutions of civil life and governance so that we can all have a seat at the table from the get-go.

Who will you bring a chair to the table for today?

Working with you to build new tables.

Eugene

# 11 November 2020

Good Afternoon

Our world places a great value on being prepared, but what are we getting prepared for?

- **It is well to be prepared for life as it is, but it is better to be prepared to make life better than it is. – Sargent Shriver**

Mr. Shriver makes a great point. It's one thing to be prepared for life as is, but it takes another kind of preparation to make life better. The former only requires an understanding of the current situation. The latter, though, takes creativity, vision, and wisdom.

I think the preparations for a better life start internally. If we want a better society, we need to prepare for it by changing ourselves. Mahatma Gandhi said it best when he said, "Be the change you want to see in the world." If we want a more just society, we must act with justice in our own way. If we want a more compassionate world, we must start by being more compassionate. If we want a more inclusive world, we must begin to act with more inclusion.

These virtues are not just for those we know; our friends, those in our own circle. We must expand our circle and start living these virtues. Change is happening all around us, and we, now, at this moment, have the opportunity to direct that change to make our world more just, compassionate, and inclusive by how we act now. This is not a bandwagon we can jump on when it becomes popular. We can't wait for "the other person" to do it first. In our own way, we all have the chance to seize the opportunity not only to prepare to make life better but make it a reality now.

How will you be preparing to make life better today?

Joined with you in not waiting for somebody else to do it.

Eugene

# 12 November 2020

Good Morning

There is a famous line from the second *Godfather* movie about keeping your friends close but your enemies closer. Maybe it's time to rethink that.

- **When you're focused on your enemy, then you are ignoring your allies. – Stacey Abrams**

I've been reading a lot in the past few days about political paybacks for those who supported or worked with the current presidential administration. Is that what we want to be thinking about at this time? I am not unfamiliar with the concept of elections having consequences, but I think political or social paybacks are not what is needed.

Maybe what Ms. Abrams is saying is that you diminish your ability to build more and better allies and alliances when you ignore your allies. If we are to become a society that is indeed a city on a hill, we need to be reaching out to each other in contradiction to the notion that it's now time for paybacks.

I think Ms. Abrams is calling us to something higher, nobler, and inevitably something more challenging. It is the easy, and maybe viscerally satisfying, thing to be able to "put people in their place." My question is, how are we ever going to create a society that breaks down isolation and that is more just, inclusive, and compassionate if all we do is shout and denounce "the enemy"?

There's no doubt that there is a great deal of hurt in our nation, and the world. Wouldn't it be a better, more fitting testimony to us as the human race if, instead of shouting at our so-called enemies with a clenched fist, we reached out to them with an open hand?

What allies will you make today?

Allied with you in reaching out with an open hand.

Eugene

# 13 November 2020

Good Morning

With COVID-19 numbers increasing, it is easy to lose hope and faith that things will get better. Things will get better; maybe all we need to do is look at each other.

- **Hope is the word which God has written on the brow of every man. – Victor Hugo**

I'm confident that Monsieur Hugo had something specific in mind when he said hope was written on everyone's brow. I think that perhaps what he is trying to say is that the only way we can really experience hope is in the face of others. In other words, we can only feel or experience hope through interaction with others.

I know it's hard to see those people that we care about due to the pandemic. I would submit that maybe it's time to start seeing hope in the faces of the people we do encounter every day: like the people in the grocery store, the letter carrier that comes every day, the overworked teacher, the exhausted healthcare worker, the discouraged cop on the beat. Maybe it's time to start exuding hope for their benefit because today, they may need it, and tomorrow, any one of us may need it.

Every time we make a phone call to somebody or write a note to a friend or greet a stranger in the street, we stand in solidarity with others to breakdown isolation and foster justice, inclusion, and compassion; and through those acts, we are showing hope on our brow. I want to think that our brows will become one big, garish, gaudy, Las Vegas style neon sign of hope the more we do these things. Maybe at this time, we need something large and gaudy.

How will you show hope on your brow today?

Celebrating with you in an ostentatious display of hope.

Eugene

# 16 November 2020

Good Afternoon

I remember the "It's Morning" campaign commercials from the 1984 presidential campaign. It's one thing to be told that it's morning, but what does it take to get up and face a new day?

- **You have to have a dream so you can get up in the morning. – Billy Wilder**

We all have our morning routines and rituals; for some, it is a shower, for others, some prayer or mediation, for others it's exercise, and for many, it's that first cup of coffee. Rituals and routines are essential in daily life, but what are the things that underpin those rituals and routines? What is it, down deep in a person's soul, that gives them the motivation to get up and get going?

Mr. Wilder contends that it's a dream, an ideal, that acts as the spark for the day. Undoubtedly, during this time of pandemic response and social and political change, it can be somewhat hard to hold on to a dream. It's enough that we get through the day.

We have expereinced almost eight months of stay-at-home orders and social distancing and hearing the COVID-19 number move in the wrong direction and listening to the political vitriol of this campaign season. Maybe now is the time to refocus ourselves from just getting by, just surviving, to reclaiming our personal dream that will not only want to make us get up in the morning but thrive, grow and be the vanguard of a new society that is more just, inclusive and compassionate.

I think that it takes a certain amount of militancy to hold onto one's dream.

There's no doubt that there are attitudes and behaviors that people would be pleased to inflict on us so that we can join in their misery. I would submit that the more we stubbornly hold onto the realistic idea of a better tomorrow, it will inspire others to join us in our obstinate hope.

Whose dream will you foster today?

Obstinately joined with you in militant hope.

Eugene

Good Afternoon

We are all living in an "instant" world. We have access to instant coffee, instant food, instant entertainment. We even have a home grocery service called INSTAcart. There is no doubt these conveniences are helpful, but what about taking the long-term view and looking to the future?

- **Someone is sitting in the shade today because someone planted a tree a long time ago. – Warren Buffett**

Now, no doubt, there is a place in our lives for things to be done immediately and expeditiously. You wouldn't want a team of firefighters standing around thinking about the long-term view before putting out your house fire. I think because of this pandemic and its response, that many of us (read: me) either get too focused on just getting through the next thing, whatever that is, or become so inwardly focused on keeping things together right now that we fail to take the long-term view.

Sooner or later, this pandemic is going to end. I have been asking myself, what I am doing now that will reap a benefit for me, the people around me, and the world in general? As I have said before, there is no going back to the "old" normal. We have to be figuratively planting trees now for the future. Maybe we won't see the restful shade those trees provide, but I am sure, that if we take the time to plant trees of inclusion, compassion, and justice, those trees will make great shade and bear bountiful fruit for others.

So … what are these so-called trees that we can plant? Every time we reach outside ourselves to somebody in pain or isolation, every time we affirm another's dignity or advocate for a community who has not enjoyed the shade that others do, we are planting a tree.

We are well past the harvest time in the northern hemisphere. We are on the brink of months of cold weather, made even colder because of the isolation. Given that, I would submit that the soil of relationships is still warm and moist and ready to be tilled.  We just need the courage to take up the plow and hoe and turn the soil.

What trees will you be planting today?

Standing side by side with you in working the fields.

Eugene

# 18 November 2020

Good Morning

I remember watching the movie *Magnum Force* and hearing Harry Callahan utter the line, "A man has got to know his limitations." I guess he never read this quote from Van Gogh.

- **If you hear a voice within you say, 'you cannot paint,' then by all means paint, and that voice will be silenced. – Vincent Van Gogh**

I am quite sure that Van Gogh was speaking about the act of putting paint on canvas, but maybe there is a deeper and broader meaning we can take from his words. I am a big believer that each one of us can "paint" our own lives. Each action we take is one more brush stroke in that painting. For some people, the painting of their lives consists of bold strokes with vivid colors. Other people's life painting is in more muted hues with meticulous brush strokes. There is nothing wrong with either approach. I think that the key that is you get the paint on the canvas.

This pandemic has caused many of us to turn inwards since our regular social interaction patterns have been disrupted, if not wrecked. I don't know about you, but when I turn inwards, sometimes the voice in my head that says *I cannot do this* gets louder.

I think the key for all of us is to recognize that voice and make the conscious decision to silence it by, as Van Gogh would say, painting. In other words, we can silence the voice, not by simply denying its existence, but by making a liar out of it and trying and doing the thing that the voice says cannot be done. Every time we make a liar out of that voice, we give it less power the next time it starts up.

This is so true with our relationship with others. Some would like to keep people separate, voices that say, *what do we have in common with "them"?* (whomever the "them" is), voices that say we cannot break the cycle of isolation that we are in or that we cannot build a better world based on justice, compassion, and inclusion. The task for us all is not to ask what we have in common but to make common cause with each other and make liars out of the voices that would separate us, whether they are external or in our own heads.

How will you paint your canvas today?

Joined with you in making common cause.

Eugene

# 19 November 2020

Good Afternoon

I was out at the grocery store earlier this week, and as it is getting colder, I saw a lot of people with their hands clenched up in their pockets, and it got me to think about the implications of being clenched.

- **You cannot shake hands with a clenched fist. – Indira Gandhi**

It could be argued that maybe Mrs. Gandhi was not speaking just about hands when she made this statement. It's one thing to have a clenched fist in a pocket to help ward off the cold, but it's another thing entirely to live a clenched life with a clenched heart.

No doubt a person can think of a thousand reasons for staying clenched, cut off, isolated from others. Many reasons might border on the petty; some reasons have their genesis in old hurts, real or otherwise. I think Mrs. Gandhi is asking us to take a risk, open our hands and hearts to the opportunities of engaging with others offers.

Sometimes, people live a clenched life as a way to protect something. Maybe that something is what they see as tried and trusted ways of living, or privileges they have enjoyed. It would indeed be the easy thing to do to simply avoid, discount, or ignore these people, but I would submit that perhaps these are the very people that are probably in dire need of somebody to reach out their open hand to them. There's no doubt that doing this engenders a good deal of risk, and there is no guarantee of success.

We all have a choice to make, and we have to make it every day. Are we going to live a life that is totally clenched or partially clenched, or are we going to live a life with an open hand, an open hand that is set to work to create a society that breaks isolation and fosters justice, inclusion, and compassion?

How will others find your hand today?

Linked with you with an open hand toward the future.

Eugene

Good Morning

I've been thinking about vision and sight the past few days and it has caused me to consider what I am looking at, what am I focusing on.

- **It is during our darkest moments that we must focus to see the light. – Aristotle**

As I was thinking about this quote, I reflected that it is easy to consider only the light that is "out there" somewhere. I started to consider not just the light that may be near or far, but my own act of focusing.

This world is full of distractions. Our focus can be shifted so quickly, but I think Aristotle is right. If we are to move to the light, to a better future, a society based on justice, inclusion, and compassion, we have to make a conscious effort to focus on that light.

Maybe a story might be more illustrative. I had the pleasure of talking with a colleague, and she told the story of how she and a friend kept from getting separated and lost on a hiking trail by shouting back and forth to each other. It took each person focusing on the other's voice to keep them both safe. No matter how much calling each person did, they would not have been able to keep each other safe without that focus.

There is a bigger question in all this. We each must decide what light we are going to focus on. Undoubtedly, each of us has our own personal spark of creativity that will allow us to blaze our own unique trail in the darkness that we are now experiencing. The question is, for each of us, to what end will that trail lead? What lights are we leaving as markers for others to focus on and follow? Are we marking a trail that is self-serving or a trail that will lead to service to others?

Maybe another story will illustrate this point. This morning, I had the opportunity to hear the story of a COVID-19 patient on the west coast of the USA who, while still intubated, got word to his wife to bring his violin. He played his violin for the doctors and nurses, and other patients on the unit, from his hospital bed. He decided to blaze his trail with music.

Each of us has those opportunities every day to blaze such a trail and leave lights as markers for others to follow and focus. Some days are harder than others for us to leave that marker. On those days, we need the markers left by others.

What lights will you leave today for others to focus?

Partnering with you in blazing new trails and leaving new lights.

Eugene

# 23 November 2002

Good Morning

Back in the day (and I am dating myself with this reference), Frank Sinatra was often referred to as "The Voice" because of his distinctive sound and excellence in singing. How will our voice be remembered?

- **A voice is a human gift; it should be cherished and used, to utter fully human speech as possible. Powerlessness and silence go together. – Margaret Atwood**

I have a friend on the east coast in the acting profession, and she refers to her voice as her instrument. This may not be an uncommon reference in the acting trade, but it got me thinking. When I think of an instrument, whether it is a surgical instrument or musical instrument, it conjures up the image of something finely crafted; something which took many hours and a great deal of skill to perfect.

Maybe that is what Ms. Atwood was thinking about when she said this. We have certainly heard many voices over the past eight months of sheltering in place and of social and political change. Still, I would ask the following question: How many of those voices were really cherished, how many of them were used to utter fully human speech and not simply shout somebody else down?

As I look out of my dining room window this bright November morning, I sense a great stillness on my street. Few people are walking, and there are no cars on the street. It's a pleasant stillness. On the other hand, I look at the houses on my street, and I wonder how much silence occurs in them. How has this pandemic silenced people's voices?

For some communities and individuals, silence is part and parcel of their daily existence, pandemic or not. Maybe it's time for us to cherish and develop our voices and advocate for the voices of others. Many stories will come out of this pandemic, and we owe it to ourselves to help the stories and voices of those who may be on the margins of society to be heard.  Through the sharing of voices, listening to others' stories and wisdom, we will break down isolation and start to move to a society based on justice, compassion, and inclusion.  I think St. Paul states it better than I can in his great discourse on love in his first letter to Corinth's Christian community.  He says, "If I speak in human and angelic tongues but do not have love, I am a resounding gong or a clashing cymbal." (1 Corinthians 13:1).

How will you cherish your voice and the voice of somebody else today?

Joined with you in rejecting the resounding gong and clashing cymbal.

Eugene

P.S. I have created a YouTube video on staying productive and connected during this time of sheltering in place.  I invite you to view it at: https://www.youtube.com/watch?v=Kyp0iaDpcmY&t=21s

Good Morning

An old saying states that if you want to get something done, ask a busy person to do it. There is a great deal of truth to that on many levels.

- **The more we do, the more we can do. – William Hazlitt**

I think there is a significant distinction to be made between being busy with work and being busy with busywork. If we are busy with work, be that what we do for a monetary wage, or if we're busy doing things around the house or taking care of ourselves, there is a certain productivity and goal in mind. But if we are busy with busywork, I think that is often an avoidance mechanism for doing things that make a difference.

The current times we are living in are forcing us to consider what is truly important and what truly needs to get done. The isolation of this pandemic, plus the onset of colder weather in the northern hemisphere and the isolation that many feel during this holiday season, could very well act as a perfect storm for some people.

I think what Mr. Hazlitt is getting at is that, as we focus on what is truly essential and do those things, we will find the inner strength, time, and wherewithal to impact people positively. However large or small, what we do to eliminate suffering, break down isolation, and help create a more just, compassionate and inclusive world will act as a beacon for others who will bring their skill, creativity, and good will to accomplish more.

How will you be busy today?

Linked with you in avoiding busywork.

Eugene

Good Morning

On this eve of the US Thanksgiving Holiday, I thought it might help reflect on gratitude for a moment.

- **Gratitude changes the pangs of memory into a tranquil joy. – Dietrich Bonhoeffer**

As many of you may know, my mom died this past April. It was not COVID-19 related as she had been ailing for some time. Tomorrow will be my first Thanksgiving without her. I'm sure that this is the first Thanksgiving without somebody significant for many people. I can still see in my mind's eye my mom arriving at my home, apron in hand, and helping get a Thanksgiving Day feast for upwards of thirty people on the table.

As I ponder this, I know I have a choice in all this. I can deeply mourn my mom's death forever, or I can be thankful for the things she and I shared and experienced together; for her wise counsel, her presence, and her work in raising me, my older brother and older sister. I think this is what Pastor Bonhoeffer is talking about. It recognizes the transformative nature of gratitude, in ways large and small, to take what might be painful and turn it into something of joy. Pastor Bonhoeffer is also correct in that the joy rendered through gratitude may not be the raucous, ebullient joy kind of joy, but a joy that is of a quiet, peaceful, and tranquil nature.

Some may look back on 2020 and say, "What do I have to be grateful for?" and that is indeed a legitimate question. Maybe part of the answer is, what have we done for others to help them answer that question? What have we done as an outward manifestation of gratitude and the tranquil joy that Pastor Bonhoeffer speaks about to break down isolation and create a new reality based on justice, compassion, and inclusion?

How will you show gratitude today and every day?

Being present to you in tranquil joy

Eugene

Good Morning

I had the chance recently to swap out my summer shirts for my winter shirts. Maybe it's not enough to swap things out for the season, but perhaps we need to be thinking about how we are wearing them.

- **If there was ever a time when one should wear life like a loose garment, this is it. – General Raymond E. Lee**

This quote is taken from General Lee's diary of 15 September 1940 when he was a military attaché at the US embassy in London. General Lee regularly walked the streets of London by day and by night, even during the heaviest air raids during the Battle of Britain.

What did General Lee mean by this statement, and what can we learn from it? Maybe what General Lee was saying was that, in the times he was living in, and perhaps by extension the times we are living, we need to be as flexible as possible. The restrictions of tight-fitting clothing or a closely scripted life aren't helpful when all manner of change is swirling about us.

A pretty convincing argument could be made around the fact that because of this pandemic, we have all manner of restrictions; that our lives in many respects have become like tight-fitting clothes. That is indeed true, but if we look beyond those restrictions, we may find all manner of opportunities to live in the freedom of a loose garment.

I would submit that this pandemic's restrictions have given us all the freedom to think differently about how we live, how we interact with people, and whom we include in our lives. We have the chance to think creatively and act creatively, from how and what we will cook in the kitchen to how we are going to build a post-pandemic society based on justice, compassion, and inclusion.

Every time we reach out to somebody to break their (or maybe our isolation), we are living life like a looser garment. Every time we use creativity to advocate for others, we are living life like a loose garment. The more we reject prejudice of all kinds, we are living life like a loose garment.

I am convinced that living life like a loose garment cannot be done in isolation. By doing what we can eliminate isolation and usher in a society based on justice, compassion and inclusion, we are helping others realize that they too can live life like a looser garment.

How will you live life like a loose garment today?

Working with you in changing the wardrobe of life.

Eugene

# DECEMBER 2020

# 1 December 2020

Good Morning

No doubt everyone has played the game where you are given a glass of water and asked what you see. Some people say the glass is half full, others say it is half empty. Some say what the person sees is a reflection of their general outlook on life. I don't know if that's true or not, but it's never too late to rethink how we view life.

- **Consult not your fears but your hopes and your dreams. Think not about your frustrations, but about your unfulfilled potential. Concern yourself not with what you tried and failed in, but with what it is still possible for you to do. – Pope John XXIII**

I know a little something about Pope John XXIII's background. He spent many years ministering in what the big shots in the Vatican (who, more often than not, discounted anything he had to say), considered the backwater of Europe: places like Bulgaria and Turkey, preaching among the dispossessed of those lands. Even as he labored in relative obscurity during those desperate years in the 1930s and 1940s, he was able to consider his unfulfilled potential.

I am convinced that each of us, even amid a pandemic and social and political change and division, still has immense potential, if only we would reject the counsel of fear that keeps us separated and isolated. Maybe this is the time to try many things to make life better for ourselves, our families, people we work with, and the world as a whole.

Pope John XXIII makes an important statement when he says to not concern yourself with what has tried and failed. Indeed, one must learn and gain wisdom from failure. I think Pope John XXIII is saying that you need not be concerned with a certain failure once you do that. Let's face it, not everything we do will come out ideally, but the important thing is to keep trying. I have always told people that I work with, especially managers, that I may come up with a hundred ideas, and ninety-nine of them might be a total failure, but that one that hits the mark will *really* hit the mark. Maybe Pope John XXIII is trying to teach us the adage about a stopped clock being right at least twice a day.

Every time we try something to make life better for somebody else, break down isolation and be the herald of a new world based on justice, compassion, and inclusion, we are tapping into that unlimited store of potential we all have. Pope John XXIII recognized that in himself, and so should we. No doubt, some days it will be more challenging than others. That's when we can help each other in shining a light in what may be a dark place; a light that guides us to more of the possible; to see more than just a half-empty glass.

What is still possible for you to do today?

Supporting you as we each fulfill our potential.

Eugene

Good Afternoon

We have all heard the phrase, "go big or go home." I think it was said in some gambling or gaming context and was even the title of a song by the group American Authors. It denotes a certain extravagance in life. I think Nelson Mandela said it better.

- **There is no passion to be found playing small – in settling for a life that is less than the one you are capable of living. – Nelson Mandela**

I believe that Mr. Mandela is making a clarion call to all of us to take the initiative to live an expansive, inclusive life. Despite this pandemic's isolation, we can, and we must, tap into our reservoir of creativity to live the life that we are capable of living.

Living the life one is capable is does not, in my opinion, mean "living large" in a superficial way. It means developing a generosity of spirit; hospitality that affirms the dignity of the other. It also means living life with passion and vigor despite the difficulties and disappointments we all face

No doubt we are in for a long, cold winter. There are some glimmers of hope concerning a COVID-19 vaccine, but that is still some time off. In the meantime, we have to find ways for us not just to survive but flourish and live as we are capable of living.

This is a time for all of us to consider who we include in our life, especially those who may have been in the margins of our life or society in general. Now is the time to think expansively on how we can be a sign of hope for others, a sign of justice, compassion, and inclusion. I am convinced that if we don't come out of this pandemic with a broader outlook on life, with a renewed commitment to really live our lives to the fullest, then all the isolation we have experienced will have been meaningless.

How will you be living the life you are capable of today?

Partnering with you in a more expansive life.

Eugene

Good Morning

I'm sorry I did not get a message out yesterday. I guess I was having trouble keeping pace. Maybe keeping pace is a sign of something else.

- **If a man does not keep pace with his companions, perhaps it is because he hears a different drummer. Let him step to the music which he hears, however measured or far away. – Henry David Thoreau**

There is a great deal of store put by "fitting in." You need only look at the nearest middle school playground to demonstrate that. I would like to think that we have grown from the middle school playground to really appreciate those who hear a different drummer. Often time, these individuals bring a fresh and unique perspective to any situation they encounter.

I wonder, though, how often do we allow ourselves to listen to a different drummer? How often do we have the courage to stand in opposition to conventional wisdom or what the "in" group advocates? How often we say that we don't have "the luxury" of being different; we have to be "the responsible voice" or "the voice of reason"?

The point I am making is that, if we can't hear our own drummer, how will we be able to appreciate those who? Being able to hear our own drummer and appreciate the drummers that others may hear is key to moving from simply tolerating others to being inclusive of others.

Life has changed radically in the past eight months. We have had to think differently about how work and business are conducted, how to gather together, and I think it also has forced us to consider who is really included in our lives. Maybe it is now that we need those different voices; those who hear a different drummer.

Maybe we need to listen to that different drummer that we have been ignoring or suppressing for too long. Perhaps we need to be that different drummer for somebody else. The more we can appreciate and rejoice in our own different drummer and other people's different drummer, the closer we will be to a more just, compassionate, and inclusive world.

How will you encourage your own drummer and those of others today?

Journeying with you, each at our own pace.

Eugene

Good Morning

I like a ride in a car as a passenger as much as the next person, especially a long ride, because I typically nod off. Being a passenger in a car or train or airplane can be fun, even exciting. But maybe being a passenger is not always desirable.

- **I have always had a dread of becoming a passenger in life. – Princess Margaret**

No doubt Princess Margaret lived a life of great wealth and privilege, but I am sure she, at times, felt overshadowed by her sister, Queen Elizabeth II. I think they call it the "heir and the spare" situation.

I think there is some wisdom we can take from what Princess Margaret said. How often in life are we simply passengers, spectators, if you will? No doubt, it is often the easy thing to do to let somebody else take the lead, to let somebody else's voice be heard. I'm not saying that one needs to be the leader all the time, but there is something to be said about ensuring that one's voice is heard clearly and distinctly.

It's a coincidence that the Gospel from this past Sunday is the story of John the Baptist, the archetype of a voice crying out the wilderness.

Let's face it, it's no fun to be the voice crying in the wilderness, but from time to time, those voices are needed. Sometimes we need to be the voice crying in the wilderness. I think that the voice in the wilderness is the ultimate example of *not* being a passenger in life.

Being a lone voice does not mean being a scold or self-righteous. Maybe speaking with a prophetic voice means calling us to really live out our potential, to be a herald of a new age.

Each one of us can be that voice. In our own way, even in this time of pandemic response and social change, we can speak with a prophetic voice for justice, compassion, and inclusion. We can move from just being a passenger in life to something fuller, something that brings out the best in all of us.

How will you be a prophetic voice today?

Partnering with you in not just being a passenger in life.

Eugene

Good Morning

There is an old saying about wearing many hats during our lifetime, meaning we all take on different roles at different times. Sometimes, some of us (read: me) go through life with many masks. That may not be the best idea.

- **We are so accustomed to disguise ourselves to others that in the end we become disguised to ourselves. – Francois de La Rochefoucauld**

I am coming to learn that the masks we put on in life can be just one more burden, a burden that is probably not necessary. Let's face it, we have enough to deal with, so why add to that with an artificial mask? Some may use a mask as a defense mechanism, and some may use a mask because they may not honestly know themselves.

I think it is a little ironic that, at a time when we are encouraged to wear a mask as a precaution, perhaps it's time to think about removing other masks. During this pandemic, I feel a tremendous sadness when I see people or myself in a mask. I feel that we are all becoming a little more isolated from each other. I can't see your smile, and you can't see mine. While wearing a mask, each of us becomes a little more than a cipher, something devoid of personality.

The physical masks we wear now are only half the story. One day, those masks will come off. At that moment, will we be ready to take off the other invisible masks that we wear? I know that down deep, each one of us can remove those invisible masks. It will take time, effort, and the willingness to take a risk. Every act of kindness, solidarity, justice, compassion, and inclusion we make is one more pull at that invisible mask.

Now is the time when we have to wear a physical mask that we should consider removing the other masks we wear. Some people will pull it off quickly, like an old bandage on a wound, some will do it gradually. The key is that we all make a start, today, to be the authentic persons we were meant to be: people affirmed in dignity and value—people without a mask.

How will you remove your mask today?

Rejoicing with you in authenticity.

Eugene

# 9 December 2020

Good Morning

Many people are familiar with the phrase from *The Rubaiyat of Omar Khayyam* that reads, "A loaf of bread, a jug of wine and thou." I think that master chef Jacques Pepin has put a more modern spin on it.

- **If you have extraordinary bread and extraordinary butter, it's hard to beat bread and butter. – Jacques Pepin**

Now, for me, nothing beats bread and butter. The key though, is to have extraordinary bread and butter. Many will say bread is bread, there is nothing so extraordinary about that, and that is where Monsieur Pepin's wisdom lies. Anything can be made extraordinary if it is done or made with care, attention to detail, vigor, and, maybe most importantly, a zest for the task at hand.

I have watched Monsieur Pepin cook many things on his various TV shows (I even had lunch with him once, along with a hundred or so other people) and the key that I take from his work is that first, he always uses quality ingredients. Second, he shows great care and focuses on his work.

So, what does that mean for us as we come to the close of a very tough year? I think the truth is that we are all capable of extraordinary things, even at this time. We all have skills and gifts that have been honed over many years of experience and many months of isolation. Now, more than ever, we need to bring those well-honed gifts and skills to create something extraordinary. We need to create a new society that is extraordinary in compassion, justice, and inclusion.

It doesn't take fancy ingredients to make extraordinary bread and butter. Fancy does not necessarily mean high quality. We may think our skills and gifts are not much to write home about, but I would beg to differ. I go back to the old bromide about the stopped clock that is right at least twice a day.

The time is *now* for all of us to say, "Yes, I have something to contribute for the betterment of myself, my family, and the people I come in contact with daily." During this time of pandemic response and social change, *everyone's* contribution is needed. Without your contribution, the loaf of bread will be lacking, and the stick of butter will be less rich.

What extraordinary skills will you bring today?

Seated with you at the table and enjoying the extraordinary bread and butter of life.

Eugene

# 10 December 2020

Good Morning

I think I am stuck in the bakery today (not for the first time and definitely not for the last time).

- **I like reality. It tastes like bread. – Jean Anouilh**

As we all know, there are different types of bread to serve different purposes and tastes. Bread is also used as a metaphor in many religious traditions. In the Roman Catholic tradition, the final Eucharist a person receives before death is called viaticum, which roughly translated means *bread* or *sustenance for the journey*. The smell of fresh-baked bread often conjures up thoughts of home. I remember going to one of the large commercial bakeries here in Chicago to pick up a donation for an annual festival and always thinking to myself, how could anyone be miserable when surrounded by the smell of all the fresh-baked bread?

Monsieur Anouilh makes an interesting analogy between bread and reality. Maybe the question he is posing is, what sort of reality are we making, what sort of bread are we making?

Go down any supermarket bread aisle, and you will see all sorts of bread, from hearty wheat and rye to what we called "cotton ball bread". Are we creating a reality for ourselves that is comparable to that cotton ball bread? Are we settling for what will just satisfy for the moment? I think the more we try to reach out to each other, to break down isolation, to offer comfort and compassion, we are, in essence, baking that hearty loaf of bread that each of us and others will be able to feed on, be nourished by and be enriched by. We will be creating the "reality bread" that people will be coming for more and more. More importantly, we will break that "reality bread" with others in justice, compassion, and inclusion.

When baking bread, especially at home, no loaf comes out the same. Each of us has a different reality, but the more we come together to share our own "reality bread," the more richness and texture will be added to our own reality. Baking bread is no trivial task. It takes skill and physical labor. I know of several people who had to give up making homemade bread because they no longer had the upper body strength to do the kneading. So it is the same with creating a robust reality for ourselves. It takes work; it takes risking being rejected by others or having one's motives questioned.

Take the chance, put in the work, make a robust "reality bread".

What sort of bread will you be baking today?

Laboring with you in the kneading and baking a new reality.

Eugene

# 11 December 2020

Good Morning

Sometimes I wonder what makes one free and what keeps one in bondage.

- **Sometimes, the thing that ties you down sets you free. – Kirk Douglas**

I had the opportunity to watch an old news story with the late veteran journalist Charles Kuralt. It was a story he uncovered in Moscow while covering the Reagan-Gorbachev summit in 1988. You can watch the story here: https://www.youtube.com/watch?v=oGwZ0pakhHE or read it in an excerpt from Kuralt's book here: https://cpb-us-e1.wpmucdn.com/sites.pc.gsu.edu/dist/6/45/files/2016/11/article-Kuralt-The-Dentist-revised-1ixiwbs.pdf.

The story is about how a group of American GIs who were POWs smuggled food to the Russian POWs who were in the same POW camp but segregated from the Americans. It is a story of comradeship, of risk and of a Russian dentist who never forgot the compassionate and ingenious Americans who were so vital to his survival and the survival of his comrades.

I thought about this in light of Mr. Douglas's statement. Here were men, deprived of all liberty, who found a freedom, a liberty, that allowed them to defy their captors and save others from sure starvation. Even though they were captives, they found a way to express freedom; a freedom that no barbed wire or stockade could restrict. It was the very fact of their captivity that set them free to hatch and execute so bold a plan.

For nearly nine months, we have been living with restrictions: masks in public, no dining out, no large gatherings, no travel. But I think that, even with these restrictions, people have been able to express freedom and liberty. Every time you reach out to somebody in compassion, you are rejecting that which would limit or restrict you as a valued, sentient human being. By the same token, when somebody reaches out to you, you are offered the opportunity to affirm your own dignity and self-worth.

What those American GIs did in a POW camp on the banks of the Oder River over seventy-five years ago took great courage. The tasks before us now, to break down isolation, to affirm our own dignity and the dignity of others, to be the herald of a world based on justice, compassion, and inclusion, also take courage. A courage found in the solitude of one's heart and spirit. I like to call this the courage of the small hours.

We have a chance now, at this moment, to take the example of those GIs and Russian POWs and reject the stockades and barbed wire around our spirit.

What ties will you be breaking today?

Laboring with you in tearing down the stockades of life.

Eugene

# 14 December 2020

Good Morning

There is an old saying about clothes making the man (or the woman). Maybe we should change that old saying to something akin to the times make the man or woman.

- **He who has done his best for his own time has lived for all times. – Friedrich Schiller**

I believe many others are putting a great store in reading the signs of the times and acting appropriately or with their best effort at that moment. Herr Schiller, on the other hand, makes a more transcendent statement about best efforts. He seems to be saying that best efforts are not only for the here and now but are for *all* times; our best efforts can directly impact *all* times.

That is indeed a serious thought: what I do now can make an impact for all times?

Without a doubt, we are all living in strange and difficult times; times that call for the best in each one of us. If one is paying any attention to the signs of the times, one can see the pain, isolation, and exclusion that many are going through.

This is what I think the heart of what Herr Schiller is saying: by doing our best now, as individuals, we can make an impact for all times. Every time we reach out in solidarity to break down isolation and help create a world based on justice, compassion, and inclusion, we are doing our best. We are not guaranteed a successful outcome, but our own personal outcomes are not that important when talking about doing one's best. Maybe the success in the effort itself. Perhaps all of our individual best efforts have a cumulative effect, which will be for all times.

How will you be doing your best today?

Working with you in reading the signs of the times.

Eugene

As we move towards the end of the Hanukkah holiday, it may be a good idea to reflect on our own individual lights.

- **For though my faith is not yours and your faith is not mine, if we are each free to light our own flame, together we can banish some of the darkness in the world. – Rabbi Lord Jonathan Sacks**

We are rushing headlong to the winter solstice here in the northern hemisphere, and it's fitting that we think about light, not just in terms of daylight (or the lack thereof) but the need for each of us to find within ourselves some light that can shine.

Each one of us has the chance to ignite a flame. For some, that ignition comes from a religious orientation, for others, a non-religious orientation. No matter what motivation causes us to ignite our own internal flame, the key is that we ACT and ignite that flame.

Acts of charity, compassion, and outreach are the flames that need to be ignited now. Rabbi Sacks provides a great insight when he speaks about being free to light our own flame. Each one of us has it within ourselves to express care differently. Just as each flame is different and one particular flame can take many forms from one moment to the next, each of us can use our expression of care as an expression of our individuality. In my opinion, it would be counterproductive if we all had to do things the same way. The beauty of Rabbi Sacks' statement is that, in our individual expressions of care and concern, we are making an indelible contribution to the whole, to the banishment of darkness.

There is a good deal of darkness to be banished. The cold and dark surrounding us will only increase and get more profound if we choose not to act; if we decide not to join our flame with the flames of others to create a world of justice, compassion, and inclusion.

It has been an absolute grind these past nine months since we all started sheltering in place, and I know (from experience) it is the easy thing to do just to hunker down and not bother lighting our own flame; to just wait it out. It may not be the easiest thing to do to reach out to others at this time. Do it anyway. I am convinced that the more we do, the easier it will become the next time and the stronger our light will be; a light that will light our way and light the way of others; a light that will encourage others, a light that will dispel darkness and cold.

How will you be kindling your flame today?

Working with you to dispel the darkness and cold.

Eugene

# 16 December 2020

Good Morning

I was recently reading about the role of influencers, mainly social media influences like the ones on TikTok. I was amazed at how many followers some of these TikTok personalities have and how rapidly they built up their following. Here is another perspective on fame.

- **On the whole, monks do not become famous – and that is a good thing – but monasteries do – and that is an excellent thing. In other words, it is the community that matters. – Basil Cardinal Hume, OSB OM**

I think it is ironic that Cardinal Hume made this statement because he eventually became the cardinal archbishop of Westminster, which made him the senior Roman Catholic prelate in England and Wales.

That being said, though, I think there is much we can learn from his statement. We all operate in various communities: communities of our family, communities at work, communities of the clubs and associations we belong to, and finally, the broader community of the world itself.

As we are moving headlong into a new year, it is a good time for taking stock not only of ourselves but also of the communities we are a part of. In this very trying year, how have we done creating and building up of community? It's an intriguing dynamic because the only way we can build up community is by caring for the community's members. Cardinal Hume understood this because he spent the better part of his adult life living in a monastic community. The Rule of Saint Benedict, which Cardinal Hume followed as a Benedictine monk, contains several chapters on service to individuals.

So, where does that leave us in the 21st Century? Some may say that the best way to serve the community is to look out for "number one". If everyone did that, we would all be better off. That's an easy way (read: cop-out) to look at it.

I am convinced that we as individuals and as a society are going to be judged by future generations on how we reacted to the extraordinary events we have lived through the past nine months. What we did, be it large or small actions, to show compassion, break down isolation, and create a world based on justice, compassion, and inclusion. We cannot leave it to "somebody else". We must draw our own line in the sand across which injustice, isolation, exclusion, and heartlessness will not cross. It's not enough just to hope for a better tomorrow. Considerable effort is needed. Even the Benedictine monks know this for their motto is *Ora et Labora*: pray and work.

How will you make the community matter today?

Joined with you in *Ora et Labora*.

Eugene

Good Afternoon

I remember my mother saying, "If everyone wanted to jump off a bridge, does that mean you want to also?" whenever I told her that, "everyone else is doing it" (whatever "it" may be). As we all know, there is a lot of wisdom in that.

- **Group conformity scares the pants off me because it's so often a prelude to cruelty towards anyone who doesn't want to – or can't – join the Big Parade. – Bette Midler**

I think that now is a good time for a bit of nonconformity, a nonconformity that will lend itself to being more open. With everything going on in the world, it's easy to just be like everyone else and wait for the pandemic's conclusion. Some may say, "Well … we have a vaccine now, so let's just wait everything out, don't rock the boat, and everyone will be fine".

This pandemic has shown some significant fault lines in our society; fault lines based on class, race, and many other aspects. I think that, for far too long, we have been willing to accept others being neglected (at best) or treated cruelly (at worst) if they didn't want to "get with the program" and join the Big Parade.

One of the great attributes of the human spirit is resiliency. We have a chance now to stand in opposition to those who would mistreat others just because they march in their own parade. We have an opportunity to create a community where all gifts are valued, and all voices are heard. We can stand in opposition to enforced conformity. Every time we reach out in solidarity to help break another's isolation, we are rejecting group conformity. Every time we accept others' outreach, we are accepting the unique gifts and dignity of another. We have an opportunity to create a society based on justice, compassion, and inclusion out of a society fraught with the efforts of those who want everyone to "know their place."

Maybe a little nonconformity and not having things all nice and tidy is the medicine we all need in addition to the COVID-19 vaccine.

How will you be creating your own Big Parade today?

Experimenting with you in some non-conformity.

Eugene

# 21 December 2020

Good Morning

During this week in 1944, the Allied forces were facing the final westward thrust of the Nazi forces in what became the Battle of the Bulge. Here is one story from that fateful battle.

To set the stage, a lone tank destroyer was retreating through the countryside when they came upon this:

- **There they found a lone soldier digging a foxhole. Armed with bazooka and a rifle, unshaven and filthy, he went about his business with a stoic nonchalance. They pulled up to him and stopped. PFC Martin, 325th Glider Infantry Rgt. didn't seem to care about the refugees. "If yer' lookin' for a safe place," he said, "just pull that vehicle behind me. I'm the 82nd Airborne and this is as far as the bastards are going. "The men on the tank destroyer hesitated. After the constant retreats of the last week, they didn't have much fight left in them. But the paratrooper's determination was infectious. "You heard the man," declared Rogers. "Let's set up for business!" Twenty minutes later, two truckloads of GIs joined their little roadblock. All through the night, men trickled in, and their defenses grew stronger. Around that single paratrooper was formed the nucleus of a major strongpoint.**
**http://www.517prct.org/documents/82nd_airborne_poster/82nd_airborne_poster.htm**

I think that sums up what a lot of us may be feeling right now. We've had a hard go of it for over nine months, on many fronts. We've put up with a lot of nonsense, heartache, and maybe even some self-doubt and self-pity. I know I have, and I have had to remember the militancy I felt when I first started doing these messages. Perhaps I needed this story to remind me of that militancy, of that commitment I made not to let this time get the better of me. Maybe we all need to remember that militancy. Perhaps we all need to start digging our own foxhole; a strongpoint where others can join. Perhaps today you will join my strong point; tomorrow I may be joining you at your strong point.

We all have a choice to make. We can either retreat alone or find a way to join with others and support each other. All it takes is for somebody to start. Somebody who is tired enough, fed up enough, and maybe just stubborn enough to say, as my friends would say, "BASTA COS SI" … *enough of this* and start digging their foxhole in the frozen December ground.

This time of year brings to mind images of home and family and gathering, goodwill, and good cheer. This is a very different holiday season. Maybe we won't be gathering like we used to, but perhaps we can all gather symbolically and support each other as we, like that infantryman of long ago, doggedly create our strongpoint, a strongpoint not only for this time, but for all times.

How will you be setting up for business today?

Digging a foxhole with you.

Eugene

Good Afternoon

Everyone has their own definition of success. For some, it is their investment portfolio's size, for some, it is fame and adulation. I remember in the 1980 and 1990s, the big thing was to have an "ego wall" where a person hung all their awards and plaques and such. A few years ago, I had the opportunity to be in the office of one of the elected officials in Cook County, and her walls were replete with plaques and awards and certificates.

Maybe at this time of year, when we take stock of the previous year, we need to be thinking of success differently.

- **If you find it in your heart to care for somebody else, you will have succeeded. – Maya Angelou**

It's easy to look back on this year with a downcast eye, given all the difficulties we have been experiencing, but maybe this is an opportunity to look back and think about how we have been able to make an expression of care for others. If we really think about it, there are no doubt countless acts of kindness, care, and solidarity that we have done in these past nine months. It's always good to take stock, take our successes where we can, and consider where we might be able to do just a little more. That marginal effort to show kindness, compassion, and solidarity may just be the thing somebody needs at that particular moment. We all need a little bit of kindness once in a while. The fact that we are receptive to the care of others helps them succeed. It may be that small success may just be the thing somebody needs at that particular moment.

We've passed the winter solstice, the shortest day of the year. That means that going forward, there will be more daylight each day. Maybe there is a lesson in that for us. As daylight increases, perhaps we can increase the light in our own lives that helps us express care, compassion, solidarity, and inclusion.

How will you increase your light today?

Joined with you in your daily successes.

Eugene

Good Morning

As I have been writing these reflections, I have noticed that on some days, the words come quickly, and on other days, it takes a little more effort. There is always that moment, though, when each of us is confronted with a blank email or a blank piece of paper, and at that moment, the opportunities are limitless.

- **The visionary starts with a clean sheet of paper and re-imagines the world. – Malcom Gladwell**

Every day can be like that blank sheet of paper. I always say that you are ahead of the game just by getting upright out of bed every day. At that moment, the potential for the day knows no bounds. At that moment, we have the potential to do good for ourselves and the people around us.

We've had nine months of getting up and choosing to do something; something good for ourselves and the people around us. Sure, we have had limits on what we can do, but even in that, people have stepped up, shown creativity, and made expressions of care, concern, and solidarity. Every day, people have gotten up and have made the clarion call for a new society based on justice, compassion, and inclusion in ways large and small. In your own way, each of you has taken up the blank sheet challenge that is every new day and re-imagined your world in ways large and small.

The key, though, is to be in it for the long haul. Maybe this pandemic has taught all of us how precious each new day really is; how important it is to make some sort of positive influence each day. It's easy to fall into a routine, a rut, as some may say. I am convinced that we need to take the lessons, some of them very hard-won, that we learned over the past nine months and, in some way, make them manifest every day.

By making those lessons manifest every day, we can become the visionaries that Mr. Gladwell speaks about and re-imagine our world into something better, into something based on justice, compassion, and inclusion.

What will you be writing on your clean sheet of paper today?

Laboring with you in re-imagining the world.

Eugene

Good Afternoon

As we are coming to the end of the year, people are starting to think about new year's resolutions, things that they want to do better next year. Perhaps it's something we should be considering all year round.

- **No matter how many goals you have achieved, you must set your sights on a higher one. – Jessica Savich**

This year, we have had to adjust many things: deferred travel and gathering with friends and family, disruptions to home, school, and work life. It seems like we all have had to take one or two steps back in many ways.

While that may be true, I know that, for me, this time has allowed me to set new goals, ones that are probably quite different from ones I had thought about before we all went to shelter in place. This time has caused me to stop and really consider the question posed in Sacred Scripture of "Who is my neighbor?" (Luke 10:29). I am confident that every religious or philosophical system asks this same question. The key for us now, is how do we respond to it? How does our response reflect our value system and the goals that we set for ourselves?

I would submit that perhaps this time of sheltering in place has influenced how we set goals in light of considering who is my neighbor? and not the other way around. In other words, instead of thinking about being in solidarity with the isolated and the marginalized through the lens of our own goals and aspirations, the desire to be of service to others, to work to break the isolation of others, to help usher a world based on justice, compassion and inclusion should become the center of our goal setting. Maybe that change in how we set goals is a higher goal that Ms. Savich calls us all to.

The beauty of this is that we don't have to wait for a new year to roll around. We can make this commitment now, and we don't just do it now; it is something we can do every day. Each new morning is a unique opportunity to be of service to others, to help in ways large and small, to alleviate suffering, break down isolation, and affirm the inherent worth and dignity of each person we meet.

How will you be setting goals today?

Striving with you for the higher goals.

Eugene

# 30 December 2020

Good Afternoon

I had the opportunity this week to have a routine medical examination that required me to fast (more or less: does Jello count?) the day before, and it gave me pause to think about fasting not only as abstaining from food but in a larger sense.

- **In anything, there has to be that moment of fasting, really, in order to enjoy the feast. – Stephen Hough**

In many ways, we have been fasting for the past nine months. We've been fasting socially and in many other ways. The question is, does this fasting have any real meaning or purpose?

I submit that maybe this time of social distancing/fasting is an opportunity for all of us. The former chief rabbi of Britain, Jonathan Sacks, said this of the fasting that occurs during the High Holy Days in the Jewish calendar: he called it a time of "prayer, introspection, and self-judgment." I think that if we look upon this time of sheltering in place as only a cross that must be borne and something to be avoided or skirted (if we can get away with it), maybe we are passing up on a golden opportunity. If we are going to be honest, self-reflection and self-criticism is not the most pleasant of activities, but it can be a great tool in self-growth.

If we learn nothing from this time, if all we do is try to resume what was a normal life, will what we have gone through have any value? During this pandemic response and social change, we have all had good days and bad days (some very bad days). I am convinced in the human spirit's ability and creativity to take what would otherwise be considered a very difficult time and turn it into something that can break down isolation, relieve suffering and usher in a society based on justice, compassion, and inclusion. It's not for me, or for anyone for that matter, to say how this will come about. It is up to everyone to find a path through this fasting to finally enjoy the feast. Sometimes the path will be a solitary one;

sometimes, it will be made easier by others' presence. In either case, I take comfort in the fact that many others are doing much the same.

How will you use your fasting today?

Patiently moving forward with you to the feast.

Eugene

# 31 December 2020

Good Morning

We've come to the end of the year, a year of extraordinary events, changes, and challenges. Some may say a defining year for this generation. The year is over, and there is nothing in the past that can be changed. But what of tomorrow? What do we have to fuel and propel us into 2021?

- **There is no medicine like hope, no incentive so great, and no tonic so powerful as expectation of something better tomorrow. – Orison Swett Marden**

I like the medicinal imagery used here. Each of us, in our own way, has had to take a powerful medicine these past nine months; a medication that, by and large, has not been the most pleasant. The question now before us is, what has this medicine wrought in each of us? I am sure that each one of us knows of people who have reacted to this medicine with a renewed hope in the future, a renewed commitment to creating a better tomorrow. The great thing about this reaction is that it can be infectious. As we all know, all it takes is one sourpuss to bring down an entire room, but the reverse is true. One person with their infectious hope and their tonic of good will can inspire a family, a community, or the world.

With the new year dawning, we have a choice to make. How are we going to react to the medicine of hope that is around us? It would be the easy thing to simply reject it, become cynical and turn inward, and use a medical term to say that the medicine is contraindicated for us. On the other hand, we can fill our prescription for the tonic of hope and let it work for us. It may take time, there may be setbacks, but in the long run, that tonic of hope will have a salutary effect on each of us, the people we come in contact with, and the world at large.

One of the benefits of the tonic of hope is that it has no memory. It is always looking forward. We may have, in the past, not been too keen on taking it. That doesn't matter. So long as we start taking it now, it will still have the full effect. It's never too late to start taking the cure and building something for a better tomorrow; a tomorrow based on justice, compassion, and inclusion, a tomorrow where the tonic of hope is not for the few but the many.

How will you be reacting to the medicine of hope today?

Imbibing with you in the tonic of a better tomorrow.

Eugene

P.S. On behalf of my wife Colleen, I want to wish you and your respective families the very best for the New Year, and a healthy, prosperous, and hope-filled 2021.

# JANUARY 2021

# 4 January 2021

Good Morning

I hope everyone had a good New Year's holiday.

It goes without saying that this past holiday season has been quite different. For many, the holidays were quieter than in years past. Maybe the quiet is not such a bad thing in that it allows us to listen more intently to what is really important.

- **Hope smiles from the threshold of the year to come, whispering, 'It will be happier.' – Alfred Lord Tennyson**

I find it interesting that Lord Tennyson speaks of the New Year whispering. Often, we get so caught up in the noise around us that the softer and often more essential voices are drowned out. We are entering into what I call the "tough" part of winter. We have no major holidays coming up, and often we (read: me) get caught in a rut, especially now while we are still sheltering in place.

I want to offer an alternative to "the rut": maybe we can take this time to appreciate the quiet, to do some active listening. Everyone will be listening for something different, but perhaps we can all try and find those voices who will be whispering, "It will be happier." Now, I am under no illusions that for a happier year to come, it will take work; a concerted effort by people of goodwill who are looking to break down isolation and create a world based on justice, compassion, and inclusion. Those voices are out there; they may be in places we don't expect, they maybe whispers we hear during the dark night of the soul or when we summon up the courage of the small hours.

Wherever we hear those voices, it is up to us to take heart, take courage, listen, and respond to those voices.

What whisperings will you hear and respond to today?

Joining with you in the smile of hope.

Eugene

Good Afternoon

Usually, this time of year is when I start "forgetting" about any New Year's resolution that I *might* have made. I'm sure that this is an indictment more on my resolution-making skills than the idea of resolutions themselves. Maybe we need a different type of resolution, something that is outwardly focused.

- **Let our New Year's resolution be this: we will be there for one another as fellow members of humanity, in the finest sense of the word. – Goran Persson**

I think Herre Persson's words are so important now more than ever. The COVID-19 pandemic has really driven home the fact that we are interdependent beings. We all need each other; maybe not today or tomorrow but one day in the not too distant future, we will need the compassion and care that others can give. It is becoming more and more apparent that we are all going to be in this for the long haul, whether we like it or not.

I have said this before, but it bears repeating. It is often the small acts of compassion and solidarity that can make the most significant difference. Simply being present to another and letting them express their fears, frustrations, fears, hopes and joy can be such a soothing balm. Those small acts often take the most courage; the courage to endure rejection or questioned motives. Take the risk anyway.

I am convinced that those who take risks now to express solidarity, to help break down isolation and work to bring about a world based on justice, compassion and inclusion, will be the ones who will have grown and developed as human beings. They will not look back on this time of pandemic response and social change, regretting the things they should have done.

How will you be there for another person today?

Joined with you in new year's resolutions that will change the world.

Eugene

# 6 January 2021

Good Morning

The New Year is always for new beginnings, new adventures, and maybe a time for forgetting, forgetting old hurts, disappointments, and fears.

- **Become so wrapped up in something that you forget to be afraid. – Lady Bird Johnson**

The question for all of us now is, what are we going to get wrapped up in? It is so easy to get wrapped up in the negative energy that is often swirling around us. There is no ignoring the fact that the times we are living in are challenging. How are we going to respond to that challenge? How are we going to keep our essential humanity? How are we going to affirm not only our own fundamental dignity, but that of others?

Each day, we have a choice in what we are going to get wrapped up in. We can choose to look out at the world and see nothing but despair and fear, or we can wrap ourselves in the knowledge that each one of us has gifts and skills that can be used to ease suffering, break down isolation and bring about a world based on justice, compassion and inclusion. Even in this time of sheltering in place and the cold of winter (at least for those of us in the northern hemisphere), we can seek out others who can help us forget about being afraid when we band together.

It does take courage. It takes courage for that first person to step out from their fear, and it also takes the courage of others to recognize that and stand in solidarity with that person.

There will always be naysayers in life, and I know the initial impulse is to reject them, but I would submit that maybe they just need a little more coaxing or handholding. I know that I have been a naysayer at times in my own life, and it was through the gentle coaxing of others I was able to change.

What will you get wrapped up in today?

Banding with you in forgetting to be afraid.

Eugene

Good Morning

I have tried not to be politically partisan in these daily messages, but I cannot let the events that occurred yesterday in Washington DC pass without comment.

- **Those who make peaceful revolution impossible will make violent revolution inevitable. – John F. Kennedy**

Every election cycle, we have had a peaceful revolution. People are elected or retained in office based on how they have worked for the electorate. Yesterday, we saw the effect of those who would thwart that peaceful revolution. I am afraid that those who would condone or in any way justify these actions are, as Winston Churchill put it, riding "to and fro upon tigers from which they dare not dismount."

The question for all of us now is how to continue the peaceful revolutions that President Kennedy spoke of. Every day, I would submit that each of us has a chance to create a peaceful revolution; not a revolution based on arms or coercion, but a revolution from inside each of us. We can daily choose to change, to reject the attitudes and actions that would foster division, exclusion, injustice, and mercilessness.

The word revolution comes from the root word revolve, meaning to move in a circle around a central axis. What are we going to have for our central axis? We have a choice. We can have an axis that states "I got mine" or an axis based on justice, compassion, and inclusion.

As we look back on yesterday's events in the nation's capital, it may be worth reflecting on something President Kennedy's brother said:

- **What has violence ever accomplished? What has it ever created? No martyr's cause has ever been stilled by an assassin's bullet. No wrongs have ever been righted by riots and civil disorders. A sniper is only a coward, not a hero; and an uncontrolled**

**or uncontrollable mob is only the voice of madness, not the voice of the people. – Robert Kennedy**

The revolution from within is very much taking the long view of history. This sort of revolution takes time and is not without setbacks, but if we want to leave any sort of legacy for future generations to build on, wouldn't it be better to leave them a foundation of those quiet interior revolutions that caused each of us in some way to turn away from selfishness and turn to care and compassion for others?

What will be your personal, peaceful revolution today?

Walking with you as we plan the revolution from within.

Eugene

Good Morning

For better or for worse, this is the 200th message that we have shared. If you had told me back in March 2020 that we would have reached this mark, I would not have believed you.

Thank you for sharing this journey with me.

By all accounts, this week has been a rough one for the United States and arguably for many in the world who look to this country as a paradigm of responsible governance and peaceful transitions of power. It may or not be coincidental, but I happened to catch part of the 1988 film *Working Girl* with Melanie Griffith, Harrison Ford, and Sigourney Weaver. The theme song from that movie is entitled *Let the River Run* by Carly Simon, and she received an Academy Award, a Golden Globe Award, and a Grammy Award for that song. The music video is worth watching: https://youtu.be/cv-0mmVnxPA. The first two lines of the song go like this:

**We're coming to the edge**

**Running on the water**

**Coming through the fog**

**Your sons and daughters**

**Let the river run**

**Let all the dreamers wake the nation**

**Come, the New Jerusalem.**

The idea of crossing a river to a new and better place is as old as history. The Old Testament records the Children of Israel's story crossing the River Jordan into the Promised Land after wandering in the wilderness for forty years. Even death is often referred to as crossing over into a better place.

I've thought a lot about this the last day or so as this song kept running through my head, and I'm thinking that we, you and I are the sons and daughters coming through the fog. We are the dreamers who are called upon to wake the nation. Being a dreamer is not just for the young. It is for everyone, both young and old. The book of the prophet Joel speaks about this: "Your sons and daughters will prophesy, your old men will dream dreams, your young men will see visions." (Joel 2:28).

It's like the song is making a clarion call to us all that, no matter how rough the river, how difficult the crossing, it is our destiny as a nation, as a people, to cross it. We don't need to wait for the waters to be calmed. We, in a united effort, the dreamers that each one of us can be, can make that crossing and build a new city, a city on a hill. In this city, all can flourish according to their talent. Isolation is broken through and through our own sweat and blood, sinew and tears, we can rend out of a wilderness a city based on justice, compassion, and inclusion.

I may sound like a starry-eyed idealist, and maybe I am. God help us if we all become jaded cynics. I am convinced that each one of us, in our own way, can add a brick or two to that city on a hill, no matter what our station in life is.

How will you awake the nation today?

Joined with you as we come through the fog and cross the river.

Eugene

Good Morning

We've heard a lot in recent months about those who have been left behind, either socially or economically, or emotionally. I think it is essential that each of us accept responsibility to ensure that nobody is left behind.

- **We don't turn back. We leave no one behind. We pull each other up. – President Barack Obama**

Now, how can we leave no one behind unless we turn back to check and see? Maybe what President Obama is saying is that we don't move backward; we don't move back to a place where we know we can be safe and leave everyone else hanging out there, exposed and on their own. Maybe what President Obama is saying is that we all need to keep our eyes on each other. Today, it's you that might be at risk of being left behind; tomorrow, it could be me. I think that what President Obama is calling us to do is listen but listen with more effort for those voices that may otherwise be drowned out; a voice calling from the wilderness.

I also think President Obama is calling upon us to make pulling one another up a personal, intimate action. It's not good enough for us to leave some provisions and a map and tell somebody to catch up when, and if, they can. President Obama is calling on each of us to pause, look to see who is falling behind, and offer a hand that they can grab. By grabbing somebody else's hand, each person becomes fundamentally involved in the destiny of others.

I think that is the call that President Obama is making. We should be looking to build a community where each individual destiny is bound up in the destinies of all.

The events of the past week shocked and horrified many. The question now before us is how to care for each other in the future so that we are bound up in each other's destiny. If we cannot ensure that nobody is left behind, if we cannot find it within ourselves to pull each other up, we will never be able to have a society that breaks down isolation and is built on justice, compassion and inclusion.

Who will you be pulling up today?

Working with you to leave nobody behind.

Eugene

# 12 January 2021

Good Morning

With the use of products like Zoom and Teams, and GoToMeeting, there has been a lot of talk about what people are wearing or not wearing during this time of virtual meetings. Maybe we can learn something from the late great Tommy Lasorda about what we are wearing.

- **I love doubleheaders. That way I get to keep my uniform on longer. – Tommy Lasorda**

I am sure that Mr. Lasorda was speaking about clothes in the narrow sense, namely his Los Angeles Dodger uniform, but I think there is a larger message to draw from this. What are we putting on every day, what are we taking off as soon as possible, and what do we like to keep wearing? I'm not necessarily talking about clothes, though. What I am talking about is attitudes, outlooks on things, behaviors.

This pandemic, and the social and political changes that are part and parcel of life these days, have caused many of us to reevaluate our beliefs, attitudes, and behaviors. I would submit that those are things that we put on every day when we get up. The question for us all is how well are they serving us now? I know it is easy to go to the "closet" and grab that old sweater or shirt that has definitely seen better days than to try and get something new.

I think that is what the challenge of these days is. To go into the "closet" of what we think and how we feel and really ask ourselves if those things are helping us through these days. There is no doubt there is much in our closet that is helpful and can be repurposed to help ourselves, our families, and the community that surrounds us, but I would venture a guess that there is still, in each of our hearts, a few things that should be cast aside.

To extend the metaphor further, I'm sure everyone has been to a rummage sale or flea market (or, as my friends in the United Kingdom might call it, a boot sale). The old saying about one man's discards is another man's treasure is entirely accurate in sales. I am convinced that the cleaning out of our emotional and mental closet is not meant to be done in a vacuum. Even with the restrictions put on us because of the pandemic, we still have ways to share ourselves with each other. I am reminded of the verse from Matthew's Gospel that speaks about the "head of a household who brings from his storeroom both the new and the old." By bringing out both the old and new from our own storerooms sharing it, we can together, forge a new world based on justice, compassion, and inclusion.

What will you be bringing out from your storeroom and sharing today?

Working with you in cleaning out the closet.

Eugene

Good Morning

There is an old saying that goes something like this: "As long as you can get upright out of bed, you are already ahead of the game for the day." I think Ralph Waldo Emerson said it better.

- **Write it on your heart that every day is the best day in the year. – Ralph Waldo Emerson**

There is no doubt that we as individuals, and as a world, are going through (and will probably continue to go through) a good deal of adversity. To some, even thinking about the days past or days ahead as the best days of the year might sound like somebody is sticking their head in the sand like an ostrich and ignoring reality. I don't think Mr. Emerson is calling for the avoidance of hardship or difficulties.

What I think Mr. Emerson is calling upon us to do is take action. Make a conscious decision to make today the best day of the year. He uses the illusion of writing it on your heart, but I think the point he is trying to make is that to make today the best day of the year requires action. It requires a choice.

Every day, the choice is to choose community over isolation, effort over inaction, and inclusion over exclusion.

I have learned from people in twelve-step programs that sobriety is achieved one day at a time, sometimes one hour at a time, and that is how we can look at making every day the best day of the year. Maybe we can think or do one thing that will make today a good day for ourselves and those around us. Human beings are endowed with a creative spark, and I am convinced that everyone with their own unique spark can make today a better day, a best day for themselves. The great thing about acting this way is that it can be contagious. The more I see others making today the best day of the year, the more I will take heart and do the same. Even with the impact of social distancing, we can hear stories of others making every day the best day of the year for themselves and others if we simply take the time, tune out the noise and listen with the heart.

How will you make today the best day of the year?

United with you in listening with the heart.

Eugene

Good Morning

No doubt there has been a lot of talk and study about cures and vaccines. Maybe it's time to think beyond just medical cures to cures for the human spirit.

- **There are no such things as incurable, there are only things for which man has not found a cure. – Bernard Baruch**

I'm sure Mr. Baruch was speaking about cures for physical ailments. In 1944, he helped fund the medical specialty we now know as rehabilitation. I think, though, that Mr. Baruch's wisdom is needed now more than ever and should be expanded to include the human spirit's ailments.

No doubt, having had to shelter in place for almost ten months now, people's spirits are becoming bedraggled and, maybe more importantly, slightly tone-deaf to the needs of others around them. I'm not saying everyone is doing that, but for some people (read: me), it takes a little more effort now to think beyond what each of us, individually, is going through.

Here is where I think Mr. Baruch's wisdom is so important: it takes the long view of history. I am convinced that people of goodwill, brought together with their skills, experiences, and gifts, can push the boundaries of what was once thought incurable: exclusion, injustice, and heartlessness.

Whether we like it or not, change is happening all around us. The question is not whether or not we want to be left behind, but what we have in ourselves to channel that change for everyone's benefit. It would be easy just to find an aspect of a particular change that works best for us and leave it at that, but I would submit that no societal change is really effective unless it can work for everyone. I don't think we should be in the business of individual cures while everyone else is left to fend for themselves.

I am confident that the cures that can lead to a world built on justice, compassion, and inclusion lie within the hearts of all people of goodwill. We just need the wisdom and fortitude to make them a reality.

What cure will you be sharing today?

Working with you in the lab to find new cures.

Eugene

# 15 January 2021

Good Morning

I have to admit that I have been doing some daydreaming recently about travel, specifically taking an Alaskan cruise, so my mind often turns to the thought of ships and sailing. I recall my parents' stories about coming to the United States via ship in the 1950s. On the eve of the Dr. Martin Luther King Jr. holiday here in the United States, maybe it is good to reflect upon Dr. King's words about being on a ship.

- **We may have all come on different ships, but we're in the same boat now. – Dr. Martin Luther King, Jr.**

Each of us, or our ancestors, came across on some sort of boat. Some came across the Bering Strait in prehistoric times, others in the genocidal middle passage in bondage, some in the steerage of ships in the 1800s, some on crafts that were less than seaworthy from southeast Asia, and in current days, people are crossing the ocean desert of the south and southwest.

However we arrived in this land, we are all part of it. Dr. King put it so pointedly that we are all in the same boat, and our destinies are bound up with each other. The question before us now is, how are we going to keep this boat from running aground? How will we keep this boat from being bashed to bits on the rocks around us? The rocks that can break up this ship are the rocks of isolation, exclusion, injustice, and selfishness.

Any boat needs a steady hand at the helm and expertise in the engine room, but I would submit that, as the crew of this ship, we can do something fundamental: we can act as a lookout. We can watch and raise the alarm of coming dangers. We can raise the alarm when a fellow crewmember is in distress. We can work together as a crew to ensure that each crew member's gifts, skills and values are acknowledged and affirmed.

It does the boat, and those on it, no good if everyone just stays in their own cabin and concerns themselves with their own cares and comforts. One member of the crew's needs should be the concern of all the crew members, and the needs of all the crew should be the concern of each individual crew member.

You and I, each one of us, make up this crew. When the history of this time is written, will it be recorded that we were all faithful lookouts?

Will you be leaving your cabin today?

Joined with you at the rail and keeping watch.

Eugene

P.S. I made a mistake in one of my earlier messages. Yesterday's message was actually the 200th message that went out. Thank you again for joining me on this journey.

# 19 January 2021

Good Morning

I try not to use Sacred Scripture directly as my basis for these reflections lest anyone think I am using them to promote my religious tradition. Still, I was at Mass this weekend, and I felt that the quotations below have value and wisdom for people of any religious tradition, or no religious tradition.

• **Samuel grew up, and the LORD was with him, not permitting any word of his to go unfulfilled. – 1 Samuel 3:19**

• **I announced your justice in the vast assembly; I did not restrain my lips, as you, O LORD, know. – Psalm 40:10**

• **Jesus turned and saw them following him and said to them, "What are you looking for?" They said to him, "Rabbi" (which translated means Teacher), "where are you staying?" He said to them, "Come, and you will see." – John 1:38-39**

Each of these scriptural passages speaks about putting oneself "out there," exposed. Samuel grew up, and no word of his went unfulfilled. The Psalmist speaks about announcing justice in the vast assembly, and Jesus is inviting his new-found followers to "come and see." Talk about being out there and exposed.

Yesterday, I had the chance to listen to some of Studs Terkel's recordings of his conversations with people on the train heading from Chicago to Washington for the March on Washington in August of 1963. During that trip, Studs spoke to quite a few people. One of them was Dr. Howard Schomer, the president of Chicago Theological Seminary at that time. He said that freedom from isolation could lead to freedom from ignorance, and a chance for solidarity.

To free others and become free from isolation takes courage. It takes the courage to let no word go unfulfilled, to announce justice in the vast assembly, and invite others to come and see.

I think about that vast assembly heading to Washington that hot August day in 1963, and I juxtapose that with the current images of our nation's capital: a capital bedecked with barricades, barbed wire, and armed troops. All, unfortunately, necessary in the times we live in.

The barbed wire and barricades won't be a permanent part of our nation's capital, and they need not be a permanent part of who we are. In our own way, each of us can announce justice, invite others to come and see so that no word of ours will go unfulfilled.

Who will you invite to come and see today?

Standing with you to announce justice in the vast assembly.

Eugene

Good Morning

Today is Inauguration Day in the United States. Today is usually marked with great oratory, but today it also marked with the memories of recent events that cannot help but color the words spoken today. One cannot reflect on a President's words without considering the political context in which they were spoken. No doubt President Abraham Lincoln is revered by many, but as we all know, he, like all of us, was no saint, but I think it is worth reflecting on his words on this day, above all others.

- **With Malice toward none, with charity for all, with firmness in the right, as God gives us to see the right, let us strive on to finish the work we are in, to bind up the nation's wounds. – Abraham Lincoln**

I think Lincoln's words ring true today as they did in 1865. Lincoln was making a clarion call then as he does now to bind up the nation's wounds, and no doubt there is a good deal of binding to do right now.

That's not to say that I think that everyone gets a pass on past behavior. I am convinced that all persons need to be held accountable for their actions. I think the task of binding the wounds would be incomplete without real justice and accountability. I've always stated in these reflections that we need to plan to build a world based on justice, compassion, and inclusion. Notice the first thing is always justice.

In my opinion, a society cannot be just if it fails to show compassion, and it can't consider itself compassionate if it fails in justice.

So, where does that leave us on this Inauguration Day? This leaves us with the task of really thinking beyond ourselves to seek out those who are hurting and are seeking justice. It's our job to come with whatever bandages and wisdom we have to truly acknowledge each human soul's fundamental humanity and value. This day charges us all to help those whose voices have been suppressed and whose full potential has yet to be realized.

The task before us is not a trivial one. We all have to get rid of some ugly images of who "the other" is if we will have any hope of moving beyond simple self-interest.

On this day, I look out the window towards the dawn on this frosty morning, with a bed of new-fallen snow. In the stillness of this morning I hear the voices of philosophers and sages of old and of our own time, calling to me to something better, to something higher: to a nation and a people, although bandaged and bruised, that is still looking and striving to be the last best hope of humanity.

Whose wounds will you be binding today?

Laboring with you to bring justice and compassion.

Eugene

Good Morning

I spent some time Wednesday watching the *Celebrating America* special last night. This may be the way future inaugurations should be celebrated. Forget the fancy balls and clothes for a select few; let's see some good music and everyday Americans. I think some of the poetry from that day is worthy of reflection. Hopefully, we will remember and reflect on it long after *we all* get down to the heavy lifting of running this country.

**Somehow we've weathered and witnessed**

**a nation that isn't broken**

**but simply unfinished - Amanda Gorman**

**But then, once in a lifetime**

**The longed-for tidal wave**

**Of justice can rise up,**

**And hope and history rhyme. - Seamus Heaney**

The poetry of Ms. Gorman and Mr. Heaney is not necessarily in opposition, but they offer different perspectives. I think that both represent a fundamental truth about our nation, and perhaps about humanity as a whole.

Ms. Gorman rightly describes us as a nation unfinished, while Mr. Heaney talks about the once-in-a-lifetime tidal wave. For all of us, the question is, what do we do while waiting for the next tidal wave? We have two choices: we can either sit around and complain about what is unfinished while we wait for the next tidal wave, or each of us, in our own way, can make those ripples on the water, both large and small, that will in some way be the harbinger of that once in a lifetime tidal way. Maybe if enough of us make those ripples on the water, we can bring about that tidal wave that would otherwise not occur.

At this time in history, I am reminded of what Adlai Stevenson the first said. He said, "As citizens of this democracy, you are the rulers and the ruled, the law-givers and the law-abiding, the beginning and the end."

It is up to all of us now, the responsibility lies within each one of us to reclaim our birthright as the rulers *and* the ruled, to not only ride the tidal wave of history but to *be* the tidal wave of history, of justice, of compassion, of inclusion. We do this all with the realization that the tasks are not easy. Nor do we with the assurance that we will live to see the ultimate perfection of our democracy. For as long as this nation stands, we will be a work in progress, and maybe that's a good thing. The fact that we will always be a work in progress means that there will always be room for people like Ms. Gorman and the countless laborers, thinkers, sages, and people of goodwill who will bring their talents and creativity to create the next tidal wave of history.

Like I said before, we have a choice. We can sit on the shore, docile, complacent, and complain or take our boat out, as unfinished and rickety as it is and find, create and ride the next tidal wave of history.

Who will you be inviting into your boat today?

Working with you to make hope and history rhyme.

Eugene

Good Morning

We're in the middle of winter, and I think that baseball is the furthest thing from most people's minds, but maybe we can draw some wisdom from home run ace Hank Aaron who died last week.

- **The pitcher has got only a ball. I've got a bat. So the percentage in weapons is in my favor and I let the fellow with the ball do the fretting. – Hank Aaron**

I was looking at Mr. Aaron's statistics, and while his number of home runs (755) is outstanding, he had 12,364 times at-bat. Over 12,300 times, he went out to the plate knowing that the percentages were in his favor. Talk about a positive attitude!

What can we learn from this? How many opportunities do we have to go to the plate, be it at home, at work, or with people we meet on the street or in the grocery store? Every time we "go to the plate" or have an interaction with somebody else, what tools do we bring? What attitudes do we present?

Each interaction we have with somebody can help break isolation and affirm somebody's essential dignity and humanity. We stand at the start of a new work week, with all its challenges. The question for us is, who are we going to let do the fretting? Are we going to let our own fears, preconceived notions, and prejudices (and there is no doubt we all have them) stop us from going to plate and using the gifts, talents, and experiences we have to help create a world based on justice, compassion, and inclusion?

Mr. Aaron has over 12,300 opportunities to bring his skill with the bat to bear. That is not the totality of who he was as a human being. We have endless possibilities to bring about healing and support to others.

The question for all of us is, how we will use the opportunities that present themselves to us every day to show care and concern? Are we going to use the tools we have and let somebody else do the fretting?

How will you be stepping up to the plate today?

Joined with you in the on deck circle.

Eugene

Good Afternoon

If you spend any time looking at real estate, you will know that people are always looking to find and move into strong, vibrant communities. Inevitably, people look to things like schools, churches, and community groups to judge a community's strength and vitality. Maybe we are looking in the wrong place?

- **When all is said and done, the real citadel of strength of any community is in the hearts and minds and desires of those who dwell there. – Everett Dirksen**

One of the challenges we all have during this time of working at home, sheltering in place and living through what I call the "heavy" part of the winter season is the tendency to become inwardly focused. We (read: me) can sometimes become more focused on what we need, what we're doing. Perhaps this is the chance we all need to think more broadly about others. Here's how I see it: we really can't (or shouldn't) be going out as we usually would, so maybe this is the opportunity we all need to take some quiet, reflective time to consider not only how to build our own personal resiliency but that of our community, however you define that.

Interestingly, Senator Dirksen uses the image of a citadel. Citadels conjure up images of fortresses; something impervious to attack, something that clearly separates "us" from "them." Maybe we need to think about citadels of inclusion, where the question is not so much "us" versus "them," but "who else" as in "who else can we include?" In this way of thinking, we move from clearly defined lines of us versus them to something more ambiguous; a question of who else can we include. As I see it, these questions are fundamental to the creation of a just, compassionate and inclusive world.

As we include more people in our citadel we all grown stronger because of the wisdom, experience, hopes and aspirations of each other.

Who will you be welcoming into your citadel today?

Joined with you in figuring out who else we can include.

Eugene

Good Afternoon

We've all seen those pictures of a person with a little angel whispering in one ear and a little devil whispering in the other ear, and the question always is, which voice will that person heed? It's a question as old as time itself.

- **Each person has inside a basic decency and goodness. If he listens to it and acts on it, he is giving a great deal of what it is the world needs most. It is not complicated but it takes courage. It takes courage for a person to listen to his own goodness and act on it. – Pablo Casals.**

What I like so much about Senor Casals' statement is that it starts from the notion that there is good in everyone. The question after that basic notion is twofold. First, how is each one of us, individually, going to respond that that voice of decency, and second, how are we going to act so that others can hear and respond to their inner voice of goodness?

I think Senor Casals would agree with me in stating that individuals (read: me) often look with suspicion on others. I know that this is something I need to work on. Let's face it; if we all are looking at each other with a jaundiced eye, it's no wonder that not enough people are responding to that basic decency that resides in all of us. We as individuals and communities need to be proactive in creating an environment where we can listen *and act on* our own goodness.

Senor Casals is also right in the fact that this takes courage. Somebody has to be the one to stand up, risk ridicule and draw a line in the sand, so to speak, that affirms the inherent dignity of the other person.

I think Senor Casals is asking for all of us to stop playing the tiresome "sweat out game" where we wait for the other person to do or say something and then laugh at them when they do.

Now, having lived on this earth for nearly fifty-seven years, I have learned something about intrigue. It is a game that many play. There will undoubtedly be people who will take advantage of those who chose to listen to their voice of decency and goodness; try to break down isolation and be the example of justice, compassion, and inclusion. Those who show courage and take the risks that Senor Casals is speaking about are, by definition, playing the long game. In the long run (and it might be a *very* long run), goodness, decency, justice, compassion, and inclusion will win out.

How will you be listening to your own voice of goodness today?

Still laboring with you in playing the long game and giving the world what it needs.

Eugene

Good Morning

Yesterday was International Holocaust Remembrance Day, when the world remembers the six million people of the Jewish faith who the Nazis murdered. I think we can learn something from the noted hunter of Nazi criminals, Simon Wiesenthal.

- **I know I am not only the bad conscience of the Nazis. I am also the bad conscience of the Jews. Because what I have taken up as my duty was everybody's duty. – Simon Wiesenthal**

These are strong words from Mr. Wiesenthal. He seems to be saying that the duty he took up to find Nazi criminals was really everyone's duty, and I think he is making an indictment of those who may have, for whatever reason, not taken up that duty.

I think that his words ring true, especially in this day and age. It is easy for any one of us (read: me) to look at the state of our community, our city, our nation, or the world and turn our backs and say, "what can I do?" or "let somebody else do it."

My friends, this pandemic has shone a bright light on the various divisions in our world. Divisions based on race, class, economics, and a myriad of other things. The questions now before us are, how do we take up the duty to bridge those divisions? We cannot go back to some sort of "previous normal" and plead ignorance. The 24-hour news cycle, for better or for worse, has ended that.

I know that each of us can make a difference in our own way. Each one of us has the skills, gifts, and, most importantly, the creativity to help build up a world based on justice, compassion, and inclusion. It's like I wrote yesterday: how are we going to respond to that voice inside each of us that is calling us to be better and do better?

I don't have all the answers; no one individual does either, but together, we can find or, if need be, create out of the battered world around us the answers we need.

To be perfectly honest, I don't want some future Simon Wiesenthal to be my bad conscience. Do you?

How will you be taking up your duty today?

Joined with you in a response to conscience.

Eugene

# FEBRUARY 2021

# 1 February 2021

Good Morning

Last week was the 35th anniversary of the space shuttle Challenger disaster. Seventy-three seconds after launch, the shuttle blew up, killing all seven crewmembers. Maybe it's worth reflecting on the words of one of those brave souls.

- **Reach for it. Push yourself as far as you can. – Christa McAuliffe**

One of the fundamental principles when navigating in space is that you don't aim directly at your target. You set your course based on where that celestial body will be some number of days in the future. With any luck, and good navigating, your trajectory and your target's trajectory will meet. Anyone who has done any hunting or shot trap or skeet will understand this principle.

What I think Ms. McAuliffe is encouraging us to do is twofold. First, she encourages us to try to exert the effort needed to push ourselves to a new reality. Secondly, and what I think is implied in her comment, is that the target we aim for is not static. Just as we as human beings are (or should be) changing, the things we are reaching for, the things we are pushing ourselves towards, are also in motion.

Another principle about good navigation is that the more data points you have, the better your navigation will be. Each one of us has the chance to be a data point for somebody else. Let me give a more concrete example. One of my favorite movies is the 1940s classic *Now Voyager* with Claude Rains and Bette Davis. In the movie, Claude Rains plays a psychiatrist, and he makes this statement: "People come to a fork in the road.

They don't know which way to go. I put up a signpost: "Not that way. This way".

The times we live in have resulted in many people (read: me) not knowing which way to go. That is where we can all put up or be a signpost for somebody else: a signpost of hope, compassion, and inclusion. If we each, in our own way, put up our own signposts, maybe the target, a world based on justice, compassion, and inclusion, will be easier to reach, no matter how far out or how hard we have to push to reach it.

What signpost will you be putting up today?

Working with you in the chart room to plot a course to a better future.

Eugene

Good Morning

Yesterday was the 18th anniversary of the space shuttle Columbia disaster. On 1 February 2003, the space shuttle Columbia broke up on re-entry over Texas and Louisiana due to wing damage incurred at liftoff. All seven of the crew died. As we reflected on one of the Challenger crew's wisdom, let's consider for a minute some wisdom from two other members of the Columbia crew.

- **When you launch in a rocket, you're not really flying that rocket. You're just sort of hanging on. – Lt. Colonel Michael P. Anderson**

- **The route to the target is more important than the target. We are going to go for the target, but we enjoy the route as well. – Colonel Ilan Ramon**

The past ten months have definitely been like riding a rocket; we have all been just holding on. I know that yesterday I spoke about laying signposts on our journey, and that has been no easy task for any of us. The hopeful thing is that, even while we have been all holding on, many people have been able to post their signposts.

We are all on this rocket together. We all need to hold onto the rocket *and* each other. In fact, by holding on to the rocket with one hand, we can, figuratively, use our other hand to reach out to somebody else or post our signpost. We need not be passive and let this rocket take us where it will. We can, by shifting weight, alter the course of the rocket. As more people "hop on" the rocket, the more we can change the course of the rocket.

I'm not sure if Colonel Anderson was speaking literally or figuratively when he spoke about hanging on to the rocket, but I am sure that there were plenty of times he was just hanging on in his life. We can decide to hang on in fear, or use the gifts, skills, and creativity we all have to use that one free hand available to reach out to somebody who may be falling off the rocket, or catch somebody adrift, or plant a signpost for somebody in the future to follow.

As we are on this rocket ride, we have another choice. Colonel Ramon speaks about enjoying the ride. There's no doubt that there's been a lot during the past ten months that has been anything less than enjoyable. Again, I know that each of us has the gifts, skills, and creativity to find enjoyment during this time. Maybe what Colonel Ramon is alluding to is that we should not be concerned just with our goals in life but the how we get there.

I've said this before: if, after this pandemic is over, we have not grown more compassionate, more inclusive, more patient, all the hardships of the past months will have been for naught. We have a choice. While we ride this rocket, we can be bitter, closed off, and apathetic, or we can find ways to be joyful and show joy to others. I've also said that, for all of us, some days will be and have been more challenging than others. It's in those moments when the others with whom we share this rocket will come to our aid. Today you may need my gifts and joy. Tomorrow (or someday in the future), I will need your gifts and joy.

How will you be riding the rocket today?

With you in enjoying the route.

Eugene

# 3 February 2021

Good Morning

I think we can all recall someone being exasperated with us while trying to explain something, and they come out with the classic line, "Are you deaf or something?". Maybe in that moment of exasperation, they are coming close to what the famous hearing-impaired actress Marlee Matlin once said.

- **The handicap of deafness is not in the ear; it is in the mind. – Marlee Matlin**

No doubt we know people who suffer from mental or spiritual blindness or deafness. The current pandemic can engender this in a person if it didn't exist already.

I know from personal experience the intense desire to wag our fingers at such people and chastise them for this. I have learned (or maybe had to relearn) the lesson that being a scold or getting indignant will not do much to eliminate the problem.

The question is, how do we combat the deafness and blindness of the mind that is pervasive in our times? Well, the first thing that is needed is silence, or as one of my relatives would say, "Shut your piehole!". No amount of talking, yelling, embarrassment or shaming is going to cure this. What's needed now is action. We need to start being the example of a world based on justice, compassion, and inclusion. We all can do something, from writing letters to address an injustice, to offering a bottle of water to the letter carrier or garbage collector we encounter at home. We need to start emulating these behaviors of justice, compassion, and inclusion to those who might not be in our regular social circle. We have a chance to make some sort of positive impact on the life of somebody else every day.

I have known people who are deaf, and I have met people who work with them. I have seen the tremendous effort they put into overcoming this handicap. Should not we be putting in the same effort to overcome mental or spiritual deafness?

How will you be listening today?

Working with you to find a cure for mental and spirituals deafness and blindness.

Eugene

Good Morning

Recently, I was watching the musical *The Music Man,* in which there is a famous scene towards the end of the movie where "Professor" Harold Hill, after he has been exposed as a fraud, gets up to direct the boy's band. Well, what came out of those instruments could only be called music in the most casual of ways. What did come out was an absolute cacophony. The interesting thing was that no matter how bad the music, the parents stood up and shouted with pride, "That's my boy!" and the boys blew their instruments with even more enthusiasm. Maybe Father Hesburgh saw that same movie.

- **The very essence of leadership is that you have to have vision. You can't blow an uncertain trumpet. – Father Theodore Hesburgh, CSC**

What I think Father Hesburgh is saying about leadership can be said about many other things in life. We have many opportunities to blow a trumpet. The question for us at this time is twofold. First, how are we going to blow that trumpet? Are we going to blow it with gusto or enthusiasm, or are we going to try and blow it with as little disruption to others as possible? The second question is maybe even more important. What will that trumpet we are blowing call us to? Will it be a call to just do the "same old same old" or will it be a clarion call to a new vision for our world: a world based on justice, compassion, and inclusion?

In this time of pandemic response and social change, there a great need for people to blow *a certain* trumpet. I know the tendency may be to wait until we have perfected our trumpet so that the sound can be the most musical, but I would submit that we need everyone's trumpet, everyone's wisdom *now*, not at some future date. Just like the boy's band in *The Music Man,* we need to make our sound heard. There will be plenty of time to refine the sound if we all work together. The key now is to get people to show up with their trumpet.

I would submit that even a trumpet that is loud and out of tune will draw people, if only to look at the spectacle. Maybe what is needed is something to bring people together and that something new and innovative can be built. I am reminded of the Bible verse, which calls us to "proclaim the word; be persistent whether it is convenient or inconvenient." (2 Timothy 4:2). The same could be said for the proclamation of justice, compassion, and inclusion.

All of us, in our own way, can sound our own unique trumpet. It may not be the most resonant sound, but it can get the job done.

How will you be blowing your trumpet today?

Joined with you in being part of the band.

Eugene

P.S. I had the honor of meeting Father Hesburgh. It's a great story. Remind me to tell you one day.

Good Morning

Today is my birthday. I have had the privilege of living fifty-seven years and sharing my life with many wonderful people. Part of the key to a good life is the ability to change. I won't say that I have enjoyed all the changes I have had to make but make them I must. Maybe part of being successful in changing is to meet the change head-on.

- **Change your life today. Don't gamble on the future, act now, without delay. – Simone de Beauvoir**

There is an urgency in what Madame de Beauvoir is calling us to. I think it is the realization that we need not play it safe all the time in life. I believe she is calling upon all of us to capitalize on the opportunities that present themselves every day to make our lives and the lives of those around us better.

If this pandemic has taught us anything, it is that there are real needs out there. People are hurting in many different ways, and I believe that each one of us has a duty in some way to change that for the better.

Not only do we have the chance to change things for others, but we can also change things for ourselves. I get the impression that Madame de Beauvoir urges us all to make the changes in our own lives with gusto and exuberance. She is not a proponent of timid change. She calls us to capitalize on the opportunities that present themselves now, at the moment, because they may not be around later.

How will you be acting without delay today?

Partnering with you in not gambling on the future.

Eugene

Good Morning

I was watching an old movie with Clifton Webb recently called *Mr. Scoutmaster*. Since February is (or at least was) Scout Month (the Boy Scouts of America was founded on February 8, 1910), I thought it might be interesting to hear some wisdom from the Scouting movement's founder.

**Try and leave this world a little better than you found it, and when your turn comes to die, you can die happy in feeling that at any rate, you have not wasted your time but have done your best. – Robert Baden-Powell**

I like the way Baron Baden-Powell put this. He says we should try to leave this world *a little* better than how we found it. It seems that he is acknowledging the fact that everyone has within their power the gifts, skills, and creativity to leave things a little better than they found them.

For each of us, the question is, when we speak about leaving things better, for whom will they be better and in what way? I don't think we will be acting in the spirit of Baron Baden-Powell's statement if all we do is make sure things are better for our little group exclusively. The key to making this world a little better might be in each of us stepping slightly out of our own comfort zone to help break the isolation we may all be feeling after eleven months of sheltering in place and take steps, however halting they are towards a world based on justice, compassion, and inclusion. I think that was the challenge in Baron Baden-Powell's time, and it is no less the challenge in our own time.

The scout motto is *Be Prepared*. We need to be prepared to capitalize on those opportunities to reach out to others. If we are so inwardly focused, we may not be able to read the signs of the times calling us to action. One of the skills taught in scouting is how to blaze a trail for others to follow effectively. There are all manner of signals that scouts learn to mark the trail for others to follow. We need to be aware of the signals that others are leaving for us to follow, and we need to leave our own signals for those that come behind us. It takes the effort of everyone to leave well-marked trails for others to follow. Without your effort, the work on the trail will, in some way, be incomplete.

What sort of trail will you be blazing today?

Laboring with you in doing our best.

Eugene

P.S. Thank you to everyone who left me birthday greetings yesterday. I had a delightful birthday topped off with some homemade apple pie. Please check out my Facebook page for pictures of the pie.

# 12 February 2021

Good Morning

As I was working at transitioning the daily messages to my personal email, I was thinking about how that can be an opportunity to do them differently. Transitions are opportunities for all of us to think and do things differently.

**Times of transition are strenuous, but I love them. They are an opportunity to purge, rethink priorities, and be intentional about new habits. We can make our new normal any way we want. – Kristin Armstrong**

Transitions, by their very nature, can be unsettling. There is a good deal of ambiguity during a time of change, be it personal or professional change. On the other hand, it is during times of change when possibilities can be limitless. As Ms. Armstrong put it, times of transition are opportunities for taking stock and re-evaluating things.

No doubt, the past eleven months have caused us all to re-evaluate things. The fact that we have all had to shelter in place may be providing the focus we need to ask and evaluate some hard questions about what we want our "new normal" to be. We all know there is no going back to the old normal. Too much has happened in the world to consider that. The key now is how do we *intentionally* create a new normal for ourselves. We shouldn't just let what we all have learned over the past eleven months be for naught and let the new normal "just happen".

We all have a chance to move boldly into a future that conquers isolation, and new social, political, and economic structures come forth that reflect the values of justice, compassion, and inclusion.

For this to happen, though, we all must do what we can, be it large or small acts. We need to be there for each other during this time of change. As Ms. Armstrong said, transitions are strenuous. Today, you may need my strength. Tomorrow I may need yours.

For better or for worse, we are all in this together. One can either resist the change or embrace it, make it our own, and thus claim our rightful stake in the new normal that we all forge together.

How will you be making a new normal today?

Joined with you in being intentional about a new tomorrow.

Eugene

# 16 February 2021

Good Morning

We had heavy snow here in Chicago last night, so that meant I was out early this morning with the snowblower trying to make a dent in it. One of my neighbors snapped a picture of me working on the snow and posted it to social media. I don't know if it was the picture's angle or something else, but I seemed very small in all that snow. Two hours later, along with some of my neighbors who came out with their shovels and snow blowers, we had a very nice path cut out. All it took was for all of us to do a little bit.

**I've found that small wins, small projects, small differences often make huge differences. – Rosabeth Moss Kanter**

As I ventured out this morning, I saw a white, frozen landscape, and it all seemed very daunting. As I got started, I had to keep in mind the capacity of the machine I was using. It has a 26-inch rake to pull in snow, but the snow was about a foot deep, so I could not use the whole twenty-six inches on each pass. I used a fraction of it, but sooner than I had expected, my driveway was clear. Then I tackled the sidewalks, and soon enough, those were cleared as well.

Each one of us in life has opportunities to achieve small wins and make small differences. Sometimes, that's all we can achieve, but those small victories should not be taken for granted. It is upon those small victories that other larger victories are built.

This pandemic has restricted us in many ways, but it has not limited our creative abilities. Creativity is key for each of us to see and capitalize on the opportunities to break down isolation and create a new society based on justice, compassion and inclusion.

These small victories need not be just things that others can see. Sometimes the small victories in terms of changes in the way one thinks or one's attitude or outlook on life can have the most lasting and profound impacts. We just need an open heart and an open mind to see them.

This morning, I saw nothing but snow, but with a few small wins and some helpful neighbors, we were all able to see a clear path.

How will you help clear a path today?

Working with you in the small projects towards the small wins.

Eugene

# 17 February 2021

Good Morning

Everyone at one time has heard the Carole King song *You've Got a Friend*. It speaks about friendship in times of adversity.

- **The friend in my adversity I shall always cherish most. I can better trust those who helped to relieve the gloom of my dark hours than those who are so ready to enjoy with me the sunshine of my prosperity. – Ulysses S. Grant**

These past eleven months have been one big basket of adversity. The question for all of us, and the one on which history will judge us is, how we respond? Did we turn inwards, or did we stand in solidarity with others?

I like to use the phrase "standing in solidarity" because it implies more than just sympathy or patting somebody's hand and saying, "there, there." It means being joined with another person in their adversity. It means taking part in their load. It means being the cherished friend of which President Grant speaks.

The cherished friend: now that's a robust descriptor. It means to protect and care for, to hold dear.

Who are we cherishing at this time? It is right and honorable to cherish those close to us, but what about those who may not be in our immediate circle? How are we cherishing those who may be on the margins of society? What are we doing to break down isolation? A person cannot be cherished if they are in isolation.

To cherish somebody, in my estimation, means to value and honor a person's inherent dignity. In the broader sense, it also means that we all need to establish institutions that will foster justice, compassion, and inclusion.

Who will you be cherishing today?

Working with you to relieve the gloom and dark hours of others.

Eugene

# 18 February 2021

Good Morning

It always amazes me how people who have gone through great suffering and adversity still manage to survive, and not just survive, but also thrive. Maybe the engine of that survival and thriving lies in their suffering itself.

- **We shall draw from the heart of suffering itself the means of inspiration and survival. – Winston Churchill**

There is a tendency in people (read: me) to avoid suffering and unpleasantness, but as one matures (read again: me), one learns that suffering is a part of life. The key is to find meaning in that suffering.

How are we to find meaning in the suffering that has been going on these past eleven months? I have concluded that any meaning we draw from this pandemic cannot be drawn in isolation. We need to find ways to connect with our fellow human beings: be they next door, in the next block, or on the next continent. By extending our hand outward to others, we can reach into their suffering and make it less omnipresent for them. Likewise, by accepting the hand reaching out to each of us, our suffering can be lessened.

I am reminded of something else Mr. Churchill once said. He said of love and smoking cigars that one should never let the fire go out. Maybe there is something in that for us in this pandemic. How have we been keeping our own fire of humanity and kindness going? I would submit that that the only way to stoke that fire is to act, and maybe even act boldly, to break down the isolation that people are enduring right now, to advocate for those who lack power and agency.

Maybe that is what Mr. Churchill is getting at. We draw from our suffering the tools we need to extend ourselves to others, to help in their suffering and thus inspire, survive and thrive.

What tools will you be drawing out today?

Joined with you in stoking the fire.

Eugene

# 19 February 2021

Good Morning

There have been countless books on happiness and how to achieve it. Maybe we are making this search for happiness too complicated?

- **If you want others to be happy, practice compassion. If you want to be happy, practice compassion. – Dalai Lama**

The use of the word practice is an aptly put phrase because it implies repetition. It also means continuous improvement through practice. There is also reciprocity in the way the Dalai Lama put it. It rejects condescension and acknowledges the equality and the dignity of both the person receiving compassion and the individual showing compassion. Finally, it illuminates that we all, at one time or other, will be on both sides of the compassion equation: the giver of compassion and the receiver of compassion.

That reciprocity is so crucial in these times because, as both the winter and the pandemic grind on, many (read: me) can be subject to what is called "compassion fatigue". Even the best of us can hear only so many stories and see so many scenes that tug at the heart. At these times, we all have to be open to receiving the care and compassion of others, and I think that we can only suitably receive that care if we know how to give it through practice.

I've stressed continuously in these messages the need to build a world based on justice, compassion, and inclusion. How are we to do that if we don't truly understand what compassion is? We can only truly understand compassion if we do both: give and receive it.

We are coming to the close of the workweek. It has no doubt been a tough week for some. Maybe this weekend, we can try, with renewed eyes, to see those who might need our compassion and become more open to those who want to show us compassion.

Compassion is like learning a foreign language. If you don't practice it, you become less fluent, and eventually, you lose any skill with it. I guess that is because compassion is indeed a new language: a language that can speak care, justice, and inclusion to a troubled world.

How will you be honing your compassion today?

Working with you at becoming more fluent in compassion.

Eugene

Good Morning

There has been considerable snowfall in metro Chicago in recent weeks that has often put a knot in trying to get around. People have had to use alternative routes. Maybe there is some value in all of us taking a different road.

- **It is dangerous to make everybody go forward by the same road: and worse to measure others by oneself. – Saint Ignatius of Loyola**

Human beings are not automatons. We are not meant to trudge mindlessly behind the person in front of us in hopes of eventually reaching some ambiguous goal.

At this time, the question is, if we are all destined to go forward by different roads, where is the solidarity in that? I think the solidarity comes when, as each of us moves forward in our own way and at our own pace, we call out to those around us. We can call out dangers that may lay ahead or places where we might come together for rest, refreshment, and mutual support. While it is true that we may go forward by different roads, no doubt paths will cross, and there will be times where people might journey together for a time on the same route.

We all need to occasionally stop along the road and evaluate what our goal is. Maybe we have spent too much time moving to a destination that is simply an illusion. That's when we need to hear others' voices on their journey and be able to read the signs of the times.

What are the signs of the times tending towards at this time? Are they tending to simply more of the same, more isolation, and a paucity of compassion and justice, or are we tending toward a world replete with justice, compassion, and inclusion?

Maybe that is what St. Ignatius is trying to lead us to. By using others' wisdom and reading the signs of the time, each of us can travel on our unique road. That road may be traversed by us alone, or it could become a broad highway for others to use. Maybe that is why St. Ignatius cautions us against measuring others by the road we are traveling.

So what, as a practical thing, can we do? I think the practice aspect of what St. Ignatius is trying to tell us is that, as difficult as it may be during these pandemic times, we need to stay connected with each other in as many ways as possible. Simply "check-in" with people, wave to strangers you may encounter as you venture outside, be more patient with others (that what I need to work on). Staying connected with others is only limited by the creativity you put into the effort.

Put in the effort. The rewards will be well worth it.

Who will you be calling out to as you travel your road today?

Supporting you as we each read the signs of the times.

Eugene

Good Morning

Yesterday would have been Senator Edward Kennedy's 89th birthday. Like most people, he was a complex person with good points and faults. The Kennedy family name conjures up opinions on a vast spectrum, but I think there is some wisdom that we can draw from his words.

**The work goes on, the cause endures, the hope still lives and the dreams shall never die. – Senator Edward Kennedy**

He said these words at the 1980 Democratic Convention. Some considered it one of the most significant political orations of its time, and Senator Kennedy referred to this line when he endorsed Barack Obama at the 2008 Democratic Convention.

What meaning do Senator Kennedy's words have for us over forty years after he spoke them? Some may look with despair at the apparent lack of progress on many fronts to build a more just, compassionate, and inclusive society. Those people may say, and with some justification, that indeed, after forty years, we should have figured it out.

This pandemic has laid bare the fact that there is still much to do. The question for us all is, what is our response? If we don't continue the work, are we making an implicit statement that the hope and dreams are dead? Are we saying there is no purpose in continuing the work?

Some may say that because dreams and hope still live, the move towards creating a new society continues. I would submit that it is the other way around. It's the work itself that spurs the hope and dreams, not the other way around. It's people who offer their sweat, blood and tears, their creativity and intellect, that are the engine for the hopes and dreams for a better world.

Perhaps that is what Senator Kennedy was getting at. He starts his statement by saying the work continues. It is the work that comes before the hopes and dreams.

The implications for us are clear. It is we who must continue the work. It is we who must break down isolation and lay the foundations for a just, compassionate, and inclusive world. It does no good to have just "pie in the sky" dreams of a utopian future. We all have a share in the work to bring hope, healing, and the affirmation of personal dignity to others.

How will you continue the work today?

Joined with you in working for the cause

Eugene

Good Morning

Yesterday, we reflected on the words of the late Senator Ted Kennedy about the dream not dying. Here is another thought on dreams that I think goes along with it.

- **Deserve your dream. – Octavio Paz**

It's only three words, but there is a lot to unpack here. I think what Senior Paz is doing is calling us all to action. It's one thing to have dreams, but to think those dreams are going to come into full bloom without any work, with no effort, is just a sense of entitlement and, let's face it, we have all seen plenty of self-entitlement in our lives (Reddit devotes pages and pages to it).

It is through work, effort, struggle, and no doubt quite a few tears, that not only do our dreams not only become a reality, but that we can take ownership of them. Think about your own life experiences about things that you were given versus those you had to break your back to achieve. Don't those things that you had to put effort into seem a little sweeter and a little more precious to you?

We all have hopes, dreams, and aspirations. Some of those dreams people around us know about, others we keep in the silence of our hearts. But what about the world around us? As a community, be it a neighborhood or city or the world, there are communal dreams: dreams for a better life for all persons, dreams of justice, compassion, and inclusion. These are no less dreams but dreams that must still be deserved, to use Senor Paz's words.

We all have a chance, now, at this moment, to contribute so that we will all deserve those dreams. Each one of us has gifts, skills, and talents that can help bring our dreams and those of the community dreams to reality.

How will you deserve your dream today?

Working with you to make the dreams of the world a reality.

Eugene

Good Morning

High school physics class was a long (really long) time ago, but sometimes, thoughts of long ago often leverage themselves into place.

- **Give me a lever long enough and a fulcrum on which to place it, and I shall move the world. – Archimedes**

For me, the essential aspect of this statement is that it takes two entirely different objects to move anything. You need both the lever and the fulcrum. Either one alone is useless.

The same is valid for life. In the case of life, it's not just two things that are needed but the myriad of wisdom, creativity, knowledge, gifts, and skills that we all bring to help shape a new and brighter future out of the pandemic and inequalities that have been laid bare by it.

Everyone's contribution is needed, and we are all diminished when somebody's gifts are missing. Maybe an example from the kitchen is relevant here. Last weekend, Colleen and I cooked a batch of beef bourguignon. The final step in the cooking is to add two tablespoons of butter mixed with flour to thicken the sauce. It never fails to amaze me how the beef bourguignon seems to come to life when those final ingredients are added. Without that butter and flour mixture, the dish would simply be some beef and vegetables floating around in a thin broth. The butter and flour add life and vitality to the dish, and so it is with everyone's contribution towards creating a more just, compassionate, and inclusive world.

What is also insightful is that butter and flour are not "fancy" ingredients. They are everyday things found in every kitchen. It is the same with how we contribute to the making of a better world. It doesn't have to be fancy. It just needs to be authentic: authentic to who you are.

Your contribution is needed, today and every day, more than ever. Your simple acts of outreach, solidarity, and compassion are now required.

How will you be adding vitality to the dish of life today?

Working with you like the lever and fulcrum to move the world.

Eugene

Good Morning

Together we have considered authenticity, but I came across a quote and a story that I think has something to tell us.

**I fear not the man who has practiced 10,000 kicks once, but I fear the man who has practiced one kick 10,000 times. – Bruce Lee**

This story is about Harry Truman's first job in Jim Clinton's drugstore in Independence, Missouri. The year was 1898:

**"I was at work at 6:30 a.m. mopping floors, sweeping the sidewalk, getting everything in shipshape when Mr. Clinton came in. In the closet under the prescription case, which faced the front and shut off the view of the back end of the store, was an assortment of whiskey bottles. Early in the morning, sometimes before Mr. Clinton arrived, the good church members and Anti-Saloon Leaguers would arrive for their early morning drinks behind the prescription case at 10 cents an ounce. They would wipe their mouths, peep through the observation hole in the front of the case and depart.**

**The procedure gave a fourteen-year old boy quite a viewpoint on the public front of leading citizens and 'amen-corner praying' churchmen.**

**There were saloons aplenty around the Square in Independence and many leading men in town made no bones about going into them and buying a drink. I learned to think more highly of them than I did of the prescription counter drinkers." – Harry S Truman**

Both Mr. Lee and President Truman are talking about the same thing: being an authentic person. Mr. Lee speaks about it in terms of learning a kick. We can all go around trying to be 10,000 different people, but the lasting impact is made if we work at being our one true and authentic self. President Truman makes a starker contrast between the people who would go into a saloon and drink versus those who bought their whiskey at the prescription counter.

I think both men have keen insight into human nature and a remarkable ability to read people. While he was in office, President Truman put great store in the American people's common sense. He contended that you could not get much over on the American people, at least not in the long run.

So it is with most of us. I'm quite confident that any one of us can recognize when we are being sold a bill of goods.

The point of all this is, if we are going to make any progress or make any contribution to the creation of a more just, compassionate, and inclusive world, what we do and how we do it must be authentic to who we are. We are only fooling ourselves if we think that trying to do these things without looking into our hearts in self-reflection will have a lasting impact. We have to be the people who are willing to practice one kick 10,000 times. We need to be the people who are willing to walk into that saloon if we want to buy a drink.

I am convinced that by showing our authenticity, others will take heart and take the risk to be authentic. Think of the implications: a society of genuinely authentic individuals, each with authentic gifts, skills, and talents offered to make the world a better place.

What will you be practicing 10,000 times today?

Learning with you to be truly authentic.

Eugene

# MARCH 2021

# 1 March 2021

Good Morning

Today is the first day of March, and as I look out the dining room window, I can see considerable thaw from the heavy snows of February. Maybe we are starting to turn the corner, not only in the weather, but in the pandemic and perhaps in our own hearts.

- **In the depth of winter I finally learned that there was in me an invincible summer. – Albert Camus**

We've all been through a pretty deep winter these past twelve months. The only way I and many others have come to bear it is to realize that there is that invincible summer within each of us, as Monsieur Camus puts it. No doubt, that summer has been covered by many things this past year, but it is still there, through it all.

For many, the fact remains that the invincible summer is still buried under the grinding isolation of this pandemic. Like in the spring, it is essential to turn over the soil in the garden so that new plants can flourish; we all have a duty to unearth the summer for those who still cannot see it for themselves.

I truly appreciate the fact that Monsieur Camus speaks about an *invincible* summer. For him and each of us, this summer is something that cannot be defeated, no matter how much snow the winter heaps upon it. It also implies permanence. This summer, a summer of the heart and mind and spirit, is something permanent within each one of us. The cares and concerns of our time may heap a lot on it, but no matter what, it is still there, as long as we, like the soil in the garden, if we are willing to do the necessary tilling so that a rich harvest can come forth.

I think some wisdom from the farm may be helpful here. On the farm, the winter is not a time of leisure. The farmer knows and makes the best use of this time for preparations for the coming growing season. The farmer knows that cold and frozen winter won't last forever, and he or she needs to be ready when and puts in the necessary work to help that invincible summer break forth.

What will our invincible summer look like when it breaks forth? Are we preparing the ground for a new summer bursting forth for all of us? One of justice, compassion, and inclusion?

How will you be helping others to uncover their invincible summer today?

Working with you to prep the soil for a new summer.

Eugene

Good afternoon

In recent years, health experts have written much about how salt can be harmful if used to excess in one's diet. That is indeed true, but sometimes we might forget that salt is a necessary mineral in our lives. It has been noted that the salinity of the blood plasma that runs through our veins is similar to seawater.

- **Let there be work, bread, water and salt for all. – Nelson Mandela**

Why does Mr. Mandela include salt in his list? The other items are ubiquitous when speaking of what people are entitled to, but why include salt? Maybe he was referring to Mahatma Gandhi's famous Salt March in March-April 1930. Mr. Gandhi used salt and the salt tax that the British Raj imposed on salt's sale as a metaphor for his people's oppression. In Matthew's Gospel, Jesus challenges His followers to be the "salt of the earth" and admonishes His followers on what happens when salt loses its saltiness (Matthew 5:13). In modern times, people often compliment others by calling them "the salt of the earth."

There may be another reason Mr. Mandela speaks of salt, one that is found in the kitchen. I have learned that all recipes, even for sweets and desserts, include a pinch of salt to help brighten and bring out the other ingredients' flavor. My wife Colleen makes wonderful pancakes from scratch (not from a mix), and she always includes a pinch of salt.

So, what does all this salty talk have to do with us at this time? Maybe what Mr. Mandela is getting at is that each of us, in our own way, must give flavor and zest to the world by our very lives. I want to think that Mr. Mandela is, in a way, challenging us. The first three items are things that we need for our survival but the last thing, no less important, is something we must give away. We must be the salt, the zest, that which brightens and brings out the flavor of life.

The salt we share is what keeps life from becoming a mere act of survival. It is what enhances and makes life anew each day that we share that salt, that zest, with others. Now, more than ever, everyone needs to bring their salt, their zest, to the world.

Just as there are different types of salt, the gifts, skills, and talents that we bring are diverse, and it is through that diversity that the world is made into something new, into a more just, compassionate, and inclusive world.

What salt will you be bringing to the world today?

Working with you to add zest to the world.

Eugene

# 3 March 2021

Good Morning

It's a bright day here in Chicago. We seem to be having a string of them, which is a good thing. It may be that we are starting to see the beginning of the end of a harsh winter and some other things equally as challenging. With the changing seasons, shadows tend to shorten

- **Keep your face to the sunshine and you cannot see a shadow. – Helen Keller**

Helen Keller was, by any measure, a prophetic voice. She could not tell the future, but she always seemed to show others a way forward despite her being blind and deaf from the age of nineteen months. By this statement, Miss Keller was able to distinguish for herself light and shadow, both in a truly physical sense and, I'm guessing, in a way that transcends the senses.

The question, the challenge for us in our own time, is how we will keep facing the sunshine. How are we going to dispel the shadows that cross our lives? There is still a great deal in our world that is beset by shadows.

The key for us is to orient ourselves physically, intellectually, and emotionally towards the sunshine. Sometimes, that sunshine is not as apparent as the sunshine I am looking at outside my dining room window. If we are going to have any hope of dispelling shadows, we need to seek out that which is positive and life-affirming.

The seeking, the journey, is also valuable because, no doubt, we will find others who are also on their journey. Each person's journey is unique, and the goals may be different, but it may be comforting to know that others are on a similar journey.

We also, like Miss Keller, must be able to speak with a prophetic voice. We must be able to help others see their way out of the shadows. We ourselves will sometimes be in the shadows and need that kind voice of

Dr. Jaquith (from the movie *Now Voyager*) to tell us "not that way, this way."

Who will you be helping out of the shadows today?

Rejoicing with you with the sun on our faces.

Eugene

# 4 March 2021

Good Morning

Recently, I went grocery shopping and was looking for some lettuce. There were all sorts of lettuces available, some heads arrayed in rows, others in bags or other containers. Some looked like they were just put out, while others looked like they would wilt by merely looking at them. The key is picking the right lettuce and keeping it crisp. The same has been said about conversation.

- **Lettuce is like conversation; it must be fresh and crisp, so sparkling that you scarcely notice the bitter in it. – Charles Dudley Warner**

Keeping things fresh and crisp is true not only of conversation but of life in general. No doubt there has been a great deal of bitterness in the past twelve months that we have all had to choke down. I think what Mr. Warner says about scarcely noticing the bitter is somewhat nuanced. He doesn't suggest avoiding the bitter or ignoring the bitter. Still, it seems to me that his call is to fill conversation, and by extension, life itself with positive and affirming energy.

Each day we get up and can choose to look for the fresh, crisp, and sparkling, or not. I know that some days it will be harder to do that than others, but in those cases, we need to use the wisdom, creativity, and care of others to point those things out. We also need to realize that there is a great deal of hurt and pain in the world. I think we each have a duty, in ways large and small, to guide others to that which is positive and affirming when they need help.

To do these things is to act and speak as a prophet. I am reminded of the biblical story of Jonah. At first, he tried to run and hide from his prophetic call, but eventually, he took up the challenge. Actions, both large and small, can be prophetic, but the key is to take advantage of the opportunities that present themselves. It is true that the pandemic has restricted us in many ways but not in *all* ways. We still can work for justice, compassion and inclusion.

How will you respond to your prophetic call today?

Working with you to keep life fresh, and crisp, and sparkling.

Eugene

Good Morning

I'm sure you have heard the phrase "snatching victory from the jaws of defeat," but there is also a similar phrase that speaks about "snatching defeat out of the jaws of victory." Maybe Nobel Laureate Dr. Ralph Bunche was considering that when he said this:

- **To make our way, we must have firm resolve, persistence, tenacity. We must gear ourselves to work hard all the way. We can never let up. – Dr. Ralph Bunche.**

The news is replete with stories of how more and more people are getting the COVID-19 vaccine, and how daily positivity rates are on the decline. I would politely submit that this is not the time to let up on the precautions people have been taking thus far. For your good and for the good of your family and the community around you, please continue with resolve and persistence in those behaviors that have kept you safe thus far: wearing a mask, social distancing, and frequent hand washing.

Not only must we act with resolve in these actions, but we also must continue to work hard to continue the changes that are going on inside each one of us as a result of this pandemic. Now is not the time to think about going back to the "old ways" of thinking and behaving.

Each of us has been given opportunities to reflect on who we are and what we value, both as individuals and society as a whole. Dr. Bunche's words are a manifestation of the fact that there is still much to do.

Destinies of peoples and communities will be shaped by how we use this time. It's not just the great and powerful that can shape destinies. We all have it within ourselves to make choices and take actions that will lead to a world that reflects justice, compassion, and inclusion.

How will you be influencing the destiny of the world today?

Resolved with you in never letting up.

Eugene

# 9 March 2021

Good Morning

I don't have a quote for you today, but I do have a news story. This week, oak trees in France were selected for use in rebuilding the spire of Notre Dame Cathedral in Paris that was ravaged by fire in 2019. (https://abcnews.go.com/International/wireStory/oak-trees-rebuild-notre-dames-spire-felled-forest-76337906).

Those acorns were planted hundreds of years ago, and the trees were to be used in shipbuilding. Some of those trees are over one meter in diameter.

The people who planted these trees were probably well aware that they would not see them harvested or used in their lifetimes. They planted them anyway.

The same can be said of the famous cave paintings in Lascaux, France. The people who made them did not know how long they would last and probably had no idea that they would be studied 15,000 years later. They painted them anyway.

The people who created the petroglyphs in the United States desert southwest didn't know how long they would last. They carved them anyway.

Every act of kindness, every time we stand in solidarity with others for justice, compassion, and inclusion, we are like those in France who planted the acorns or the cave dwellers who created the paintings or carved the petroglyphs. We don't know what fruit will be borne by our actions or when it will be harvested. We all must take a risk, a risk without the certainty of a positive outcome or *any* outcome. We'll have to trust that the kindness, justice, compassion, and inclusion we show now will bear fruit for somebody else to harvest in the future.

What acorns will you be planting today?

Partnering with you in creating a bright legacy for the future.

Eugene

Good Morning

I got a real lesson in patience this morning. I was trying to register for a COVID-19 vaccine and got to the last screen, only to be shut out at the last moment. I was ready to pull my hair out. I went for some exercise on the treadmill after this and had the chance to watch the beginning of the movie *Lilies of the Field*. I took special note of Homer Smith and Mother Maria's scene where they are sitting at the table looking at the Bible and swapping verses about the worker being "worthy of his hire." It's pretty apparent from that scene that Homer wants to get paid and make a fast break out of there, but Mother Maria has other ideas. Mother Maria uses a good deal of subterfuge to get Homer to build her chapel, but I think it's her patience combined with Homer's hard work that gets the job done.

**There is no substitute for hard work, twenty-three or twenty-four hours a day. And there is no substitute for patience and acceptance. – Cesar Chavez**

Mr. Chavez makes an important point. It's not good enough to simply be patient, to wait around for something to happen. Work is required; sometimes arduous, sometimes tedious, but work nevertheless.

That is the dynamic we find ourselves in now. We are all waiting for the pandemic to be over; we are all looking to what the "new normal" will be but in the meantime, there is still work to be done. Work that we have to do to grow as human beings. Work that we as a community have to do to build a more just, compassionate, and inclusive world. We even have to work to get scheduled for a COVID-19 vaccine.

If I have learned anything over these past twelve months, it's that patience and acceptance, linked with hard work, go a long way to help make the isolation a little more bearable and, I believe, help drive away the bitterness that some people might be feeling because of it.

I am always amazed how a little patience goes a long way and how it can defuse an otherwise tense and upsetting situation. We (read: me) have to be patient with each other and, most importantly, patient with ourselves. The extra kindness and consideration that we (read: me) need to show ourselves is vital if we are to be patient and kind to others.

Many things in our world desperately need changing, and sometimes the rate of change can seem glacial, but here is where the hard work *joined* with patience can make such a difference.

How will you be patient with yourself and others today?

Joined with you in hard work *and* patience.

Eugene

# 11 March 2021

Good afternoon

There is an old saying here in Chicago that there are two seasons: winter and road construction. With the coming of warmer weather, I know several people embarking on construction projects of various sizes. What are we doing about our own personal construction?

- **Each of us is carving a stone, erecting a column, or cutting a piece of stained glass in the construction of something much bigger than ourselves. – Adrienne Clarkson**

I want to think that each day, every one of us has the chance to add to that construction that is bigger than any individual. Some days, we might be adding some ornamentation, while other days, we might be adding a beam or column that will go unseen by all but is vital to the integrity of the building.

Building something, whether it is a garden shed, a magnificent palace, or a world based on justice, compassion, and inclusion, should not be just "thrown together" if there is to be any hope of it being permanent. It takes thoughtful planning and input from many people. Also, it takes many different skills to bring about a successful construction project. It is also true for the "new normal" that we want to come out of this pandemic. Each of us, in our own way, has skills, gifts, and talents that are needed, and without them, the project, in some way, is diminished.

It might be said that these past twelve months have been one big construction season for all of us. Many of us (read: me) are trying to think and act in different ways. Many are trying to create new institutions that better serve all of humanity. We all know that some days the work will be more challenging than others. In those times, we need to look to others' support to lend us the tools we need to carry on. Many times that tool might be a kind word, a smile, or an act of compassion. Today you may need it, and tomorrow I may need it.

Whatever construction we are participating in, it is vital to continue to carve the next stone, put up the next column, or cut the next piece of stained glass until the job is done. To do otherwise is to be left with a half-constructed life, a half-constructed world.

How will you be adding to the construction today?

Joined with you in sharing the tools for building a better world.

Eugene

Good afternoon

Does anyone remember the TV show *Lifestyles of the Rich and Famous*? I think that is the show that was the forerunner of modern reality TV and the contemporary fascination (some might say obsession) with celebrity and the "wealthy" lifestyle. Undoubtedly, this show promoted one perspective of wealth, but Ambassador Andrew Young offers another view of wealth.

- **I have about concluded that wealth is a state of mind, and that anyone can acquire a wealthy state of mind by thinking rich thoughts. – Andrew Young**

What does it take to have a wealthy state of mind? I think that it has to do with what we are putting into our minds. Now, let's face it, I am all for a good binge on occasion of some mind-numbing Netflix series. We all need that, but we cannot make a steady diet of it.

This year has given us all a chance to rethink many things, including how we choose to entertain ourselves. Rich thoughts are the byproduct of our entertainment choices and how we think about and interact with others. It's true that our personal interactions are severely limited, but isn't that all the more reason to make those interactions we can have meaningful and rich?

The diversity in people's experiences and our ability to be open to them is another aspect of thinking rich thoughts. This past year has made me realize how fragile life can be and how frayed the ropes binding us together as human beings can become. Having a mindset of abundance and rich thoughts can only help strengthen those bonds.

If we are ever to move beyond a veneer of justice, compassion, and inclusion, we need to be thinking deeply and richly about who we are and our place in the world.

Now that we are starting to see the light at the end of this long pandemic tunnel, we (read: me) need to start thinking about a rich and radical hospitality. I don't think we can wait until we are out of the tunnel and then say to ourselves, "what now?" If we do that, some people (read: me) might fall back into that comfortable one-dimensional thinking that gave us *Lifestyles of the Rich and Famous.*

How will you be thinking richly today?

Planning with you a rich and radical hospitality.

Eugene

Good Morning

I've been watching the movie *Lilies of the Field* while on the treadmill this week. Many people are fascinated with Homer Smith's (the character played by Sidney Poitier) relationship with Mother Maria, the character played by Lilia Skala. In contrast, I have become interested in another character in the film, specifically Juan Aquilito, played by Stanly Adams.

We first see Juan fixing Homer breakfast while the nuns are at Mass. Homer asks him why he isn't at Mass, and he says this:

**Praying does not pay the rent and praying does not fill up the gas.**

**God ain't gonna get behind this counter and sling hash.**

**Me? I gotta fill my wallet.**

This is a statement of complete self-interest. As long as Juan can fill up the gas and his wallet, things are good.

Later in the firm, he is seen helping Homer build the chapel. He says this to Mr. Ashton as to why he and the others are helping Homer:

**Mr. Ashton: Say, where'd you get all the material?**

**Juan: The people give them, Senor.**

**Mr. Ashton: What for?**

**Juan: A man, he gives wood... bricks. In time, what does he get? A chapel... a place where his children can receive the sacraments. To these men, for their children to have faith, it is important.**

**Mr. Ashton: Is that why you're here?**

**Juan: To me, it is insurance. To me, life is here on this earth. I cannot see further, so I cannot believe further. But, if they are right about the hereafter, I have paid my insurance, Senor.**

Juan still has a good deal of self-interest, but he has moved from being disinterested to participating in the effort to build the chapel

Finally, we see Juan dressed in his best suit, giving Father Murphy, the itinerant friar who celebrates Mass in the area, a tour of the chapel and pointing out to him the bricks he set with his own hands above the door.

Now, I have no idea if Juan found any religious faith by helping build the chapel, but I see how Juan has transformed as a person because he moved from isolation to involvement. Maybe there is a lesson in there for us.

If we are to make any progress in creating a world based on justice, compassion, and inclusion, we (read: me) cannot look upon that which we do for others as simply "buying insurance" for the hereafter or as a basis for keeping score. During this pandemic, we all have an opportunity to fundamentally change how we relate to others, not just others who are like us.

The expressions of care we make now can move us from doing them out of a sense of obligation to a deeper motivation; a motivation born out of who we are becoming. I have seen this in my own life. There are things that I do, not out of a sense of obligation, but because to not do them would be a betrayal of who I am. I am not saying that I am the paragon of virtue, but I am on the journey like all of us. I don't know where this journey will take me or when or where it will end, but I do know that if I am to travel it, it may mean leaving things like keeping score or "paying my insurance."

Insurance is a good thing in some cases. It can help mitigate risk and help provide financial stability, but when it comes to personal growth and creating a new and better world out of this pandemic, maybe what is needed is more risk-taking. I'm not talking about financial risk but the risks of the heart, the risk of being vulnerable, and responding to other people's vulnerability.

What will you be leaving behind today on your journey of growth?

Journeying with you as we cancel our insurance policies.

Eugene

Good afternoon

It's tax season here in the United States, and I know that many people are looking at their deductions, especially charitable contributions. Businessman and philanthropist Walter Annenberg also thought about contributions.

- **You will not be satisfied unless you are contributing something to or for the benefit of others. – Walter Annenberg**

I am sure what Mr. Annenberg was speaking of was contributions that don't wind up on a tax form. I think he was talking about contributions that come from the generosity of spirit.

The pandemic has, to quote a friend of mine, "worked on my last good nerve," and I think the risk we run is that, while we can see the light far off in the distance that marks the end of the pandemic, we are not there yet and we still must press on towards it. How are we to keep pushing on towards that light?

One way is to remember the stories of grace under pressure that we have seen and heard. We need to remember our journey and the contributions we have already made, both large and small, to benefit others during this pandemic.

In physiology, there is something called "muscle memory" that states if you repeat an action enough times, the action can be completed with little or no conscious effort.

Just like a brisk workout can leave you physically satisfied, working out those charitable impulses and building not muscle memory but spiritual memory can also lead to the satisfaction that Mr. Annenberg speaks.

Maybe that is what we need now. We need to be exercising those instincts of justice, compassion, and inclusion to such an extent that they become second nature, and to do otherwise would seem foreign or unnatural to us.

How will you be creating spiritual memory today?

Partnering with you in becoming satisfied.

Eugene

# 17 March 2021

Good Morning

One of my favorite movies is *Marty*. Ernest Borgnine, who plays the title character, received the Academy Award for Best Actor in 1955. There is a scene early in the film where Marty is sitting with his friend Angie, and they are trying to figure out what to do on a Saturday night. They go back and forth with the line, "I dunno, what do you want to do?" Neither of them is willing to put a stake in the ground and make a move. Perhaps the great opera singer Marian Anderson met many similar people.

- **There are many persons ready to do what is right because in their hearts they know it is right. But they hesitate, waiting for the other fellow to make the first move - and he, in turn, waits for you. – Marian Anderson**

The pandemic has caused us to have to wait for many things; many revolve around gathering together for holidays, significant events, or just enjoying each other's company.

On the other hand, the pandemic has not limited us from doing the right thing regarding how we relate to each other. I would submit that it is *vital* that we try and be that person who makes the first move, who makes the first move towards justice, compassion, and inclusion.

I am convinced that none of us need to wait for somebody else to make the first move to break down the months of isolation this pandemic had wrought. I had the chance to read an article in yesterday's *Wall Street Journal* about people who are ministering to the crews of cargo ships who cannot leave the ship when in port. This expression of care and concern is emblematic of the creativity that people can muster when called up. We all have that well of creativity to drill into to help ameliorate the isolation and "the blues" we feel because of twelve months in isolation.

I know the need out in the world is so great, but all it takes is for one person to make the first move, to put a stake in the ground in some way, be it large or small, to relieve suffering and be a sign of hope for somebody else.

How will you be making the first move today?

Working with you to put the stake of hope in the ground.

Eugene

Good Morning

I see the reports of the violence wrought in Atlanta this week, and I feel so impotent. I wonder if we as human beings have learned nothing. I sit hear reaching for words, and nothing comes easily. Maybe all that is needed is for humans to continue to stand against evil.

- **Thou shalt not be a victim, thou shalt not be a perpetrator, but, above all, thou shalt not be a bystander. – Yehuda Bauer**

Every day, we are confronted with evil and the effects of injustice. What is the appropriate response? Some may call for more "law and order," but I am uncertain that strictly punitive measures will work. It's like trying to lash down the safety valves on a boiler. You may prevent an explosion, but eventually, those valves will fail.

So what is there for us to do? I think the key lies in what Professor Bauer says. We cannot be bystanders. If we are ever to have any hope of progressing as humans, we have got to start thinking about how we stand in solidarity with those who are the objects of violence and injustice. I have no simple formula for you to follow. Each person must find their own path to solidarity. Each person must find their own voice to speak up for justice, compassion, and inclusion.

It is only when we have found our voice and path that we move from bystander to actor. Shakespeare said that "all the world is a stage." He does not refer to an audience.

The time is now to use what agency we possess to speak and act to move from bystander to actor. It is not enough that we have simply bought our ticket for the performance. We have to mount the stage and act.

All this does not come without risk, but let's face it, every day we get upright out of bed is a risk. Isn't it worth one more risk to help bring about true, lasting, and meaningful change and comfort to our world?

How will you find your voice today?

Working with you on the next act of the performance.

Eugene

Good Afternoon

Today marks one year that we started on the journey with these daily messages. I want to thank you for your support in accompanying me on this journey.

- **Anniversaries are like birthdays: occasions to celebrate and to think ahead, usually among friends with whom one shares not only the past but also the future. – Zbigniew Brzezinski**

- **May you live all the days of your life. – Jonathan Swift**

Anniversaries engender a lot of reminiscing, and sometimes people (read: me) tend to look at those memories with a certain nostalgia; through the prism of rose-colored glasses. While that might be nice to do, sometimes it can inhibit us from 1) looking at those bygone years realistically and 2) truly moving forward. We have seen in our own society the loud and strident desire of some to return to a bygone era. In this era, they, and people like them, may have been very comfortable, but others suffered injustice and discrimination. Those people conveniently forget about that, but we shouldn't.

That is why it is so important to look at the past realistically.

Now, the question for us is, how will we look back on this past year? We need to remember both the fun and silly things we did (often on Zoom) to break the monotony, but we also need to remember the trials many people went through and the human costs of this pandemic.

By remembering this past year, realistically, we can lay a true and solid foundation for the future: a future based on justice, compassion, and inclusion.

It is here where Mr. Swift and Mr. Brzezinski's statements come together. By being realistic and honest about our past and using that to build a foundation for the future, we can live each day we are given. We move from just getting by, mere survival, to flourishing.

This year has taught us many hard lessons; we owe it to ourselves to truly live each day. What that means is different for each person, and the arc of discovery is part and parcel of living each day fully, with zest, and most importantly, with integrity.

How will you be thinking ahead today?

Striving with you to live each day with zest and integrity.

Eugene